Key Stage 3

Mathematics
Levels 4–6

Revision Notes

Author
Fiona C Mapp

Series editor
Alan Brewerton

EDUCATIONAL

Every effort has been made to trace copyright holders and to obtain their permission for the use of copyright material. The authors and publishers will gladly receive information enabling them to rectify any error or omission in subsequent editions.

First published 1998
Reprinted 1998 (five times)
1999 edition first published 1998

Letts Educational, Schools and Colleges Division, 9–15 Aldine Street, London W12 8AW
Tel. 0181 740 2270
Fax 0181 740 2280

Text © Fiona C Mapp 1998

Editorial, design and production by Hart McLeod, Cambridge

British Library Cataloguing-in-Publication Data
A CIP record for this book is available from the British Library

ISBN 1 84085 180 5

Printed and bound in Great Britain by Ashford Colour Press, Gosport

Letts Educational is the trading name of BPP (Letts Educational) Ltd

Acknowledgements
The author and publishers are grateful to the staff at Cottenham Village College, Cambridge, for their technical assistance.

Contents

Preparing for your Key Stage 3 SATs

You may remember taking National Tests (often called SATs) in Science, English and Maths when you were about 7 and 11 years old. Your Key Stage 3 SATs, taken in May at the end of Year 9, are the last National Tests that you will take before your GCSE examinations in two years' time.

The Key Stage 3 SATs are important because they help show how much you have improved in these three important subjects. They will also help you, your parents and your teachers plan ahead for your GCSE courses next year. Your teachers may use the results of your SATs to help place you in the most appropriate teaching group for some of your GCSE courses.

It is, therefore, a good idea to be well prepared when you take your SATs. Good preparation will lead to good marks and increased confidence. This is where this book is of value.

How to use this book

This book will help you prepare for your SATs in the easiest possible way. It is clearly divided into National Curriculum topics which you will have covered during the past three years. The information is presented as a series of facts, explanations and examples which will help to refresh your memory and improve your understanding.

The book also contains useful tips and advice from examiners which show you how to avoid common mistakes and improve your marks. There is also space for you to make your own notes and comments. Each section finishes with a short test so that you can check that you have covered the topic sufficiently.

Your SATs are important, and this book gives you an excellent opportunity of making the most of them.

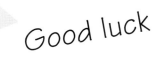 Good luck

Number and algebra

Place value and the number system

Numbers

Each digit in a number has a **place value**.

The size of the number depends on its place value.

The place value changes by a factor of 10 as you move from one column to the next.

40

The place value is **ten** for this digit 4.

ten millions	millions	hundred thousands	ten thousands	thousands	hundreds	tens	units	
						6	2	sixty two
					5	3	8	five hundred and thirty eight
				4	2	9	2	four thousand two hundred and ninety two
			5	3	4	0	0	fifty three thousand and four hundred
		2	3	6	5	2	0	two hundred and thirty six thousand five hundred and twenty
	4	3	9	5	0	2	5	four million, three hundred and ninety five thousand and twenty five

These gaps make big numbers easier to read.

Always read the numbers from left to right.

Rounding numbers to the nearest, ten, hundred, thousand

Large numbers are often approximated to the nearest ten, hundred, thousand etc.

Rounding to the nearest ten

Look at the digit in the **units** column.
If it is less than 5, round down.
If it is 5 or more, round up.

Example
Round 568 to the nearest ten.

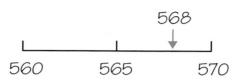

568 is closer to 570 than 560.

There is an 8 in the units column, so round up to 570.

Rounding to the nearest hundred

Look at the digit in the tens column. If it is less than 5, round down. If it is 5 or more round up.

Example
Round 2650 to the nearest hundred

There is a 5 in the tens column, so round up to 2700

2650 is 2700 to the nearest hundred.

Rounding to the nearest thousand

Look at the digits in the hundreds column. The same rules apply as before.

Example
Round 16420 to the nearest thousand.

Sketch a number line if it helps.

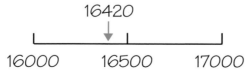

There is a 4 in the hundreds column, so round down to 16000.

16420 is 16000 to the nearest thousand.

Directed numbers

- These are numbers which may be **positive** or **negative**. Positive are above zero, negative are below zero.

- Negative numbers are commonly used to describe temperatures, i.e. −3 °C means 3 °C below zero.

Examples

−4 is smaller than 4.

−2 is bigger than −5.

Example

Arrange these temperatures in order of size, smallest first.
−6 °C, 4 °C, −10 °C, 3 °C, 2 °C, −1 °C

Arranged in order: −10 °C, −6 °C, −1 °C, 2 °C, 3 °C, 4 °C.

Adding and subtracting directed numbers

- When adding and subtracting directed numbers it is helpful to draw a number line.

Example

The temperature at 3 p.m. was 2 °C; by 11 p.m. it had dropped by 7 °C. What is the temperature at 11 p.m.?

Drawing a number line often helps.

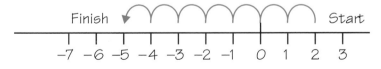

The new temperature is −5 °C.

Example

Note the different uses of the minus signs.

Find the value of $-2 - 7$ (note the different uses of the minus sign).

$$-2 - 7$$

This represents the sign of the number, i.e. start at -2.

This represents the operation of subtraction, i.e. Move 7 places to the left.

Finish ⌒⌒⌒⌒⌒⌒⌒ Start

−9 −8 −7 −6 −5 −4 −3 −2 −1 0

- When the number to be added (or subtracted) is negative the normal direction of movement is reversed.

Example

$-6 - (-1)$ is the same as $-6 + 1 = -5$.

The negative changes the direction.

Move 1 place to the right.

- When two (+) signs or two (−) signs are together then these rules are used:

Care needs to be taken with these types of questions as they can be difficult.

$$\left.\begin{matrix} +(+) = + \\ -(-) = + \end{matrix}\right\}$$ **Like** signs give a **positive**.

$$\left.\begin{matrix} +(-) = - \\ -(+) = - \end{matrix}\right\}$$ **Unlike** signs give a **negative**.

Examples

$$-2 + (-3) = -2 - 3 = -5 \qquad -4 - (+4) = -4 - 4 = -8$$

$$5 - (-2) = 5 + 2 = 7 \qquad 6 + (-2) = 6 - 2 = 4$$

Negative numbers on the calculator

The $\boxed{+/-}$ or $\boxed{(-)}$ key on the calculator gives a negative number.

For example, to get −2, press $\boxed{2}$ $\boxed{+/-}$ or $\boxed{(-)}$ $\boxed{2}$.

This represents the sign.

Example

$$-6 - (-3) = -3$$

is keyed into the calculator like this:

$\boxed{6}$ $\boxed{+/-}$ $\boxed{-}$ $\boxed{3}$ $\boxed{+/-}$ $\boxed{=}$

sign   operation   sign

Check that you know how to enter it on your calculator.

Fractions

- A fraction is part of a whole one.
  $\frac{2}{5}$ means 2 parts out of 5.

- The top number is the **numerator**, the bottom one is the **denominator**.

- A fraction like $\frac{2}{5}$ is called a **proper fraction**.

- A fraction like $\frac{12}{7}$ is called an **improper fraction**.

- A fraction like $1\frac{4}{9}$ is called a **mixed number**.

> If the numerator and the denominator are the same then it is a whole one, i.e. $\frac{6}{6} = 1$.

Equivalent fractions

- These are fractions which have the same value.

Example

$\frac{1}{2}$ $\frac{2}{4}$

From the diagram it can be seen that:

$$\frac{1}{2} = \frac{2}{4}$$

- Fractions can be changed into their equivalent by either **multiplying** or **dividing** the numerator and denominator by the same amount.

Examples

$$\frac{7}{9} = \frac{?}{27}$$

$$\frac{35}{50} = \frac{7}{?}$$

> This method can be used to simplify fractions.

$\times 3$

$\frac{7}{9} = \frac{21}{27}$

$\times 3$

Multiply the top and bottom by 3.

$\div 5$

$\frac{35}{50} = \frac{7}{10}$

$\div 5$

Divide the top and bottom by 5.

Using the fraction key on the calculator

$a^b/_c$ is the fraction key on the calculator.

Example

$\frac{20}{30}$ is keyed in as [2] [0] [$a^b/_c$] [3] [0].

This is displayed as 20⌐30 or 20⌐30.

The calculator will automatically cancel down fractions when the [=] key is pressed. For example, $\frac{20}{30}$ becomes 2⌐3 or 2⌐3.

This means two-thirds.

A display of 1⌐5⌐7 means $1\frac{5}{7}$. If you now press [shift] [$a^b/_c$], it converts back to an improper fraction, 12⌐7.

Check: your calculator may have a [2nd] or [Inv] key instead of [Shift].

Decimals

- A decimal point is used to separate whole number columns from fractional columns.

Example

Thousands	Hundreds	Tens	Units	Tenths	Hundredths	Thousandths
6	7	1	4 • 2		3	8

decimal point

- The 2 means 2/10.
- The 3 means 3/100.
- The 8 means 8/1000.

Remember, hundredths are smaller than tenths, i.e. $\frac{3}{100}$ is smaller than $\frac{2}{10}$.

Recurring decimals

- A decimal that **recurs** is shown by placing a dot over the numbers that repeat.

Example

$0.66666\ldots = 0.\dot{6}$ $0.147147\ldots = 0.\dot{1}4\dot{7}$

Ordering decimals

When ordering decimals:

- First write them with the same number of figures after the decimal point.

- Then compare whole numbers, digits in the tenths place, digits in the hundredths place, and so on.

Example

Arrange these numbers in order of size, smallest first:

4.27, 4.041, 4.7, 6.4, 2.19, 4.72.

First rewrite them:

4.270, 4.041, 4.700, 6.400, 2.190, 4.720.

Then reorder them:

2.190   4.041   4.270   4.700   4.720   6.400.

Have a quick check that all values are included.

the zero is smaller than the two.

Rounding numbers

Decimal places (d.p.)

When rounding to a specified number of decimal places:

- Look at the last digit that is wanted (if rounding 8.347 to 2 d.p. look at the 4 (second decimal place).

- Look at the number next to it (look at the number not needed, i.e. the 7).

- If it is **5 or more** round up the last digit (7 is greater than 5, so round the 4 up to a 5).

- If it is **less than 5**, the digit remains the **same**.

Examples

16.5**9** = 16.6 to 1 d.p.

8.43**5** = 8.44 to 2 d.p.

12.3**4** = 12.3 to 1 d.p.

Percentages

These are fractions with a **denominator of 100**.

For example 62% = $\frac{62}{100}$.

Equivalences between fractions, decimals and percentages

Fractions, decimals and percentages all mean the same thing but are just written in a different way.

Fraction	Decimal	Percentage
$\frac{1}{4}$ $1 \div 4$	0.25 $\times 100\%$	25%
$\frac{6}{10}$	0.6	60%
$\frac{1}{6}$	$0.166\dot{6}$	$16.6\dot{6}\%$

Ordering different numbers

When putting fractions, decimals and percentages in order of size, it is best to change them all to **decimals** first.

Example

Place in order of size, smallest first:

$\frac{1}{4}$, 0.241, 29%, 64%, $\frac{1}{3}$

0.25, 0.241, 0.29, 0.64, 0.3$\dot{3}$ Put into decimals first.

0.241, 0.25, 0.29, 0.3$\dot{3}$, 0.64 Now order.

0.241, $\frac{1}{4}$, 29%, $\frac{1}{3}$, 64% Now rewrite in its original form.

Make sure you put the values in the order the question says.

Index notation

- An **index** is sometimes known as a **power**.
  6^4 is read as **6 to the power 4**. It means $6 \times 6 \times 6 \times 6$.
  5^6 is read as **5 to the power 6**. It means $5 \times 5 \times 5 \times 5 \times 5 \times 5$.

  a^b known as the **index** or **power**.

  known as the **base**

- The **base** is the value which has to be multiplied. The **index** indicates how many times.

Powers on a calculator display

The value 5×10^6 means $5 \times 10 \times 10 \times 10 \times 10 \times 10 \times 10$

$$= 5\,000\,000.$$

On a calculator display 5×10^6 would look like $\boxed{5\;^{06}}$.

On a calculator display 7×10^{19} would look like $\boxed{7\;^{19}}$.

Place value and the number system

Questions

1 The temperature inside the house is 12 °C warmer than outside. If the temperature outside is −5 °C. What is the temperature inside?

2 Work out what the missing letters stand for:

(a) $12 - A = -3$.   (b) $-6 + 10 = B$ (c) $-8 - (D) = 2$ (d) $14 + (F) = -6$

3 Working out the missing values:

(a) $\frac{7}{12} = \frac{14}{x}$ (b) $\frac{125}{500} = \frac{y}{100}$ (c) $\frac{19}{38} = \frac{76}{z}$

4 The weights of some objects are:

2.7 kg, 19.4 kg, 6.032 kg, 6.302 kg, 2.74 kg, 19.04 kg.

Arrange the weights in order of size, largest first.

5 Write out fully:

(a) 2^5 (b) 7^3 (c) 8^4

6 Jonathan's calculator display shows, $\boxed{1.52 \ ^{06}}$. Write down what the calculator display means.

7 Write 24% as a fraction in its simplest form.

8 A flag is coloured red (27%), blue (61%) and the rest is yellow. What percentage is yellow?

9 Change these fractions into (a) a decimal, (b) a percentage:

(a) $\frac{7}{9}$ (b) $\frac{2}{3}$ (c) $\frac{3}{5}$ (d) $\frac{4}{16}$

10 Round 6.493 to 2 decimal places.

11 Round 12.059 to 2 decimal places.

12 Round 9.47 to 1 decimal place.

13 Write the number 3,248,020 in words.

14 Round these numbers to the nearest 10

(a) 62   (b) 55   (c) 128

15 Round these numbers to the nearest 100

(a) 146   (b) 289   (c) 1350

16 Round these numbers to the nearest 1000

(a) 7449   (b) 8826

Relationships between number and computation methods

Using a calculator

Order of operations

Bodmas is a made up word which helps you to remember the order in which calculations take place.

B o D M A S

Brackets over Division Multiplication Addition Subtraction

This just means that brackets are carried out first then the others are done in order.

Examples

$(2 + 4) \times 3 = 18$ $6 + 2 \times 4 = 14,$

not 32 because multiplication is done first.

Important calculator keys

$(-)$ or $+/-$ Change positive numbers to negative ones.

C This only cancels the last key you have pressed.

AC This cancels all the work.

$a^{b/c}$ This key allows a fraction to be put in the calculator.

$\sqrt{}$ Square root button.

x^2 Square button on some calculators.

Shift 2nd Inv These allow 2nd functions to be carried out.

When using a calculator:

- Press the keys slowly and carefully.

- If the incorrect key is pressed, clear it by using C instead of AC.

- Always press the = key after each calculation.

Example

$$\frac{\sqrt{32} + 6.5}{4.9} = 2.41 \text{ (2 d.p.)}$$

Check that you obtain this answer on your calculator.

Estimates and approximations

- A good way of checking answers is by estimating. Numbers are usually rounded to the nearest 10/100/1000, etc.

Example

A tin of cat food weighs 58 g; estimate the weight of 306 tins.

$$58 \times 306 \approx 60 \times 300 = 18\,000$$

- $\approx$ means approximately equal to.

A quick way of multiplying 60×300 is $6 \times 3 = 18$, then place 3 zeros on the end, $18\,000$.

Types of number

Multiples

These are just the numbers in multiplication tables. For example, multiples of 6 are 6, 12, 18, 24, . . .

Factors

These are whole numbers which divide exactly into other numbers. For example, factors of 12 are 1, 2, 3, 4, 6, 12.

Prime numbers

Make sure you know the prime numbers up to 20.

These are numbers which only have 2 factors, **1 and itself**. Prime numbers up to 20 are

2, 3, 5, 7, 11, 13, 17, 19.

Note that 1 is not a prime number.

Squares and cubes

- Anything to the **power 2** is **square**. For example, $3^2 = 3 \times 3 = 9$.

- Anything to the **power 3** is **cube**. For example, $4^3 = 4 \times 4 \times 4 = 64$.

Square numbers include:

1	4	9	16
1 × 1	2 × 2	3 × 3	4 × 4

Square and cube numbers can be represented by a diagram.

Cube numbers include:

1   8   27

  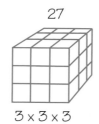

1 x 1 x 1   2 x 2 x 2   3 x 3 x 3

Square roots and cube roots

$\sqrt{}$ is the **square root sign**. Taking the square root is the opposite of squaring, for example, $\sqrt{36} = 6$ since $6 \times 6 = 36$.

$\sqrt[3]{}$ is the **cube root sign**. Taking the cube root is the opposite of cubing, for example, $\sqrt[3]{64} = 4$ since $4 \times 4 \times 4 = 64$.

Multiplication and division by 10, 100, 1000

To **multiply** by 10, 100, 1000 etc., move the decimal point one, two, three etc., places to the right, or put in zeros if necessary.

Examples

15.2 x 10 = 152   Move the decimal point one place to the right.

53 x 10 = 530   Put in a zero.

15.2 x 100 = 1520   Move the decimal point two places to the right.

53 x 100 = 5300   Put in two zeros.

15.2 x 1000 = 15200   Move the decimal point three places to the right.

53 x 1000 = 53000   Put in three zeros.

To **divide** by 10, 100, 1000 etc., move the decimal point one, two three etc., places to the left.

Examples

15.8 ÷ 10 = 1.58   56 ÷ 100 = 0.56   18.2 ÷ 1000 = 0.0182

When multiplying by multiples of 10 (20, 30, 700 etc.) the same rules apply, except you multiply the numbers first then move the decimal point to the right.

Examples

50 x 30 = 1500
24 x 20 = 1480

When dividing by multiples of 10, the same rules apply, except you divide the numbers and then move the decimal point to the left.

Examples

6000 ÷ 20 = 300
930 ÷ 30 = 31

Four rules of number

You need to be confident when using the four rules of number.

Examples

$$
\begin{array}{r}
2471 \\
628\ + \\
\hline
3099 \\
\end{array}
\qquad
\begin{array}{r}
36\overset{5}{4}\overset{1}{8} \\
1152\ - \\
\hline
2496 \\
\end{array}
\qquad
\begin{array}{r}
473 \\
6\ \times \\
\hline
2838 \\
\end{array}
\qquad
\begin{array}{r}
108 \\
6\,\overline{\smash{)}\,64\overset{4}{8}}
\end{array}
$$

Always make your working clear.

Long multiplication

Example

A single plant costs 42p. Without a calculator work out the cost of 164 plants.

42p each

$$
\begin{array}{r}
164 \\
42\ \times \\
\hline
328 \\
6560\ + \\
\hline
6888 \\
\end{array}
$$

Step 1: 164 x 2
Step 2: 164 x 40
Step 3: 328 + 6560.

Cost = 6888p or £68.88.

Make your working out clear.

Long division

Example

A vase costs 74p. Tracey has £9.82 to spend. What is the maximum number of vases Tracey can buy? How much change does she have left? Do this calculation without using a calculator.

Remember to change the units first.

$$
\begin{array}{r}
13 \\
74\ \overline{\smash)98\,2} \\
74\ - \\
\overline{242} \\
\underline{222} \\
20
\end{array}
$$

Step 1: 74 goes into 98 once, put down 1.

Step 2: Place 74 below 98.

Step 3: Subtract 74 from 98.

Step 4: Bring down the 2.

Step 5: Divide 74 into 242, put down the 3.

Step 6: 74 x 3 = 222.

Step 7: 242 – 222 = remainder 20.

Tracey can buy 13 vases and has 20p left over.

Calculations with decimals

Examples

When adding or subtracting decimals make sure they have the same number of place values, i.e. 4.9 = 4.90.

Add together 6.21 and 4.9.

$$
\begin{array}{r}
6.21 \\
4.90 \\
\hline
11.11
\end{array}
$$

Put the decimal points under each other.

This is the same as 4.9

The decimal point in the answer will be in line.

Subtract 6.2 from 12.81.

$$
\begin{array}{r}
12.81 \\
6.20\ - \\
\hline
6.61
\end{array}
$$

The decimal points are in line.

$$
\begin{array}{r}
12.3 \\
7\ \times \\
\hline
861
\end{array}
$$

Multiply 123 by 7 = 861, ignore the decimal point.

Since 12.3 has 1 number after the decimal point then so must the answer.

Answer = 86.1.

$$\begin{array}{r} 4.3 \\ 6 \overline{\smash{)}25.8} \end{array}$$

When dividing, divide as normal, placing the decimal points in line.

Put the decimal points in line.

Fractions

Fractions of a quantity

• The word **of** means **multiply**.

Example

In a class of 40 students $\frac{2}{5}$ of them are left-handed. How many are left-handed?

$\frac{2}{5}$ of 40 means $\frac{2}{5} \times 40 = 16$ students.

On the calculator key in

$\boxed{2} \quad \boxed{\div} \quad \boxed{5} \quad \boxed{\times} \quad \boxed{40} \quad \boxed{=}$

This can be worked out by dividing 40 by 5 to find $\frac{1}{5}$ and then multiply by 2 to find $\frac{2}{5}$.

Percentages

Percentage of a quantity

• The word **of** means **multiply**.

Replace the word **of** with a × sign. Rewrite the percentage as a fraction.

Example

Find 15% of £650.

$\frac{15}{100} \times 650 = £97.50$.

On the calculator key in

$\boxed{15} \quad \boxed{\div} \quad \boxed{100} \quad \boxed{\times} \quad \boxed{650} \quad \boxed{=}$

• If working out mentally, find 10% = 650 ÷ 10 = £65. 5% is half of £65 = £32.50. Add the two together to give £97.50.

Example

Work out $17\frac{1}{2}\%$ of 360 without a calculator.

$$10\% \quad \text{of } 360 = 36$$
$$5\% \quad \text{of } 360 = 18$$
$$2\frac{1}{2}\% \text{ of } 360 = \quad 9$$

So $17\frac{1}{2}\%$ of $360 = 36 + 18 + 9 = 63$.

One quantity as a percentage of another

- To make the answer a **percentage** multiply by **100%**.

Example

A survey shows that 26 people out of 45 preferred 'Supersuds' washing powder. What percentage preferred Supersuds?

$$\frac{26}{45} \times 100\% = 57.\dot{7}\% \text{ (1 d.p.)}$$

On the calculator key in

| 26 | ÷ | 45 | × | 100 | = |

Make a fraction with the two numbers. Multiply by 100% to get a percentage.

Proportional changes with fractions and percentages

- Fractions and percentages often appear in real life problems.

Example

The table shows some information about pupils in a school.

	Not vegetarian	Vegetarian
Girls	147	62
Boys	183	41

There are 433 pupils in the school, (147 + 62 + 183 + 41).

(a) What fraction are vegetarian?

(b) What percentage of the pupils are boys?

(a) Vegetarian = 62 + 41 = 103

   Fraction $= \frac{103}{433}$

(b) Percentage of boys: $\frac{224}{433} \times 100\% = 51.7 = 52\%$.

Example

BEANOZ
225 g

The tin of baked beans holds 225 g. During a sales promotion 12% extra is added. How many grams of beans are now in the tin?

$\frac{12}{100} \times 225 = 27\,g$ Work out 12% increase.

New amount of beans is 225 + 27 = 252 g.

Add the increase onto the original weight.

Ratio

A ratio is used to compare two or more related quantities.

- **Compared to** is replaced with **two dots** :

Sharing a quantity in a given ratio

- Add up the total parts.

- Work out what one part is worth.

- Work out what the other parts are worth.

Example

A forest covers 25 000 hectares. Oak and ash trees are planted in the forest in the ratio 2 : 3. How many hectares do the ash trees cover?

A quick
check is by
working out
the number
of hectares
the oak
trees cover.
The total of
the oak + ash
should be
equal to
25 000
hectares.

   2 + 3 = 5 parts.

   5 parts = 25 000 hectares.

   1 part = $\frac{25\,000}{5}$ = 5 000 hectares.

Ash has 3 parts, i.e. 3 × 5 000 = 15 000 hectares.

Relationships between number and computation methods

Questions

1 Without a calculator work out:

(a) $4 \times (2 + 3)$ (b) $6 + 4 \times 5$

2 Work out the following without a calculator:

(a) $\begin{array}{r} 6214 \\ 298+ \\ \hline \end{array}$ (b) $\begin{array}{r} 6351 \\ 2170- \\ \hline \end{array}$ (c) $\begin{array}{r} 3259 \\ 7\times \\ \hline \end{array}$ (d) $6\overline{)1290}$

3 1   2   3   4

5   6   7   8

9   10   11   12

From the above numbers write down:

(a) Any multiples of 3.

(b) Any prime numbers.

(c) Factors of 20.

4 Work out the following

(a) $\dfrac{5.6 + 3.2^2}{1.8}$ (b) $\dfrac{\sqrt{50} + 6^2}{2}$

5 Work out without a calculator:

(a) $\sqrt{100}$ (b) 6^2 (c) $\sqrt{36}$ (d) 2^3

6 Without a calculator work out:

(a) 15.2×10 (b) 6.3×100 (c) 21×1000 (d) $25.2 \div 100$

7 A tin of soup costs 68p. Work out the cost of 18 tins without using a calculator.

8 The cost of a trip is £10.25. If Mr Appleyard collects in £133.25 how many people are going on the trip? Work out without using a calculator.

9 Out of a class of 31, 12 are left-handed. What percentage are left-handed?

10 A jumper costs £30. If it is reduced in the sale by 15%, how much does it now cost?

11 5/8 of a class of 24 walk to school. How many pupils walk to school?

12 Ahmed and Fiona share £500 between them in the ratio 2 : 3. How much does each receive?

Solving numerical problems

Calculations

- When solving problems the answers should be rounded sensibly.

Example

$12.1 \times 4.6 = 55.66 = 55.7$ (1 d.p.)

Round to 1 d.p. since the values in the questions are to 1 d.p.

Example

James has £15.36. He divides it equally between 5 people. How much does each person receive?

$£15.36 \div 5 = £3.072$
$= £3.07.$

Round to £3.07 since it is money.

Interpreting the calculator display

- When questions involve money the following points need to be remembered:

  a display of $\boxed{6.7}$ means £6.70 (Six pounds seventy pence),

  a display of $\boxed{5.03}$ means £5.03 (Five pounds and three pence),

  a display of $\boxed{0.82}$ means £0.82 or 82 pence,

  a display of $\boxed{6.2934}$ needs to be rounded to 2 d.p., i.e. £6.29.

Checking calculations

- When checking calculations the process can be reversed like this.

$102 \times 6 = 612.$ Check $612 \div 6 = 102.$

$\times 6$

102   612

$\div 6$

Trial and improvement

- This is when successive approximations are made in order to get closer to the correct value.

Example

If $12x - x^2 = 34$, use trial and improvement to find the value of x to 1 decimal place.

Draw a table to help.

Substitute different values of x into $12x - x^2$.

> Remember x^2 means x times x.

x	$12x - x^2$	Comment
3	$36 - 9 = 27$	too small
4	$48 - 16 = 32$	too small
5	$60 - 25 = 35$	too big
4.5	$54 - 20.25 = 33.75$	too small
4.6	$55.2 - 21.16 = 34.04$	too big
4.55	$54.6 - 20.7025 = 33.8975$	too small

> Remember it is the value of x which is the answer, i.e. 4.6 not 34.04.

At this stage the solution is trapped between 4.5 and 4.6. Checking the middle value $x = 4.55$ gives $12x - x^2 = 33.8975\ldots$ which is very close to 34.

```
        4.5            4.55           4.6
   (too small)    (too small)   (just too big)
```

The diagram shows that even though 4.6 is slightly too big it is the closest solution to 1 decimal place.

Best buys

- Unit amounts are looked at to decide which is the better value for money.

Example

£1.06   £2.81

The same brand of breakfast cereal is sold in two different sized packets. Which packet represents the better value for money?

- Find the cost per gram for each packet.

  125 g = £1.06   Cost of 1 g = 106 ÷ 125 = 0.848 p.

  750 g = £2.81   Cost of 1 g = 281 ÷ 750 = 0.3746 p.

- Since the 750 g packet costs less per gram, it is the better value for money.

Time

12 and 24 hour clock times

The **12 hour clock** uses **a.m.** and **p.m.**
a.m. means **before midday**, p.m. means **after midday**.

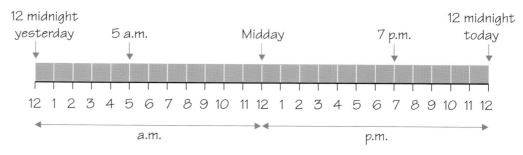

The **24 hour clock** numbers the hours from 0 to 23. It is written using four figures.

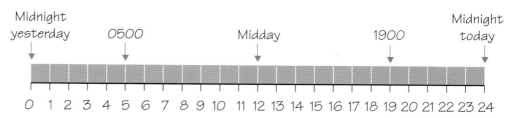

You need to be able to write times using both the 12 hour and 24 hour clock.

Remember to write in 'a.m.' and 'p.m.' for 12 hour clock times.

Examples

2:42 p.m. is the same as 1442.   1534 is the same as 3:34 p.m.

4:30 a.m. is the same as 0430   0904 is the same as 9:04 a.m.

Timetables

Timetables often use 24 hour clock time. Timetables should be read carefully.

Example

The train timetable illustrates the train times from London to Manchester.

There will a train from London every 60 minutes i.e. 0750, 0850.

If the timetable is written in 24 hour clock times, make sure your answers are in 24 hour clock times.

London Euston	0602	0650	Every 60	1100	1300
Watford Junction	0632	0720	minutes	1130	1330
Stoke on Trent	0750	0838	until	–	1445
Manchester Piccadilly	0838	0926		1315	1540

The 0750 train from Stoke on Trent.

The 0650 train from London arrives in Manchester at 0926.

The 1100 from London Euston does not stop at Stoke on Trent.

(a) Diana is travelling from Watford Junction to Manchester, Piccadilly. If she catches the 0602 train, how long is her journey?

(b) If I arrive at London Euston at 1142, how long do I have to wait for the next train to Manchester?

(a) 0632   →   0838   Time = 2 hours 6 minutes
   Depart   Arrives
   Watford   Manchester
   Junction

(b) The next train is at 1300 hours. I must wait:

   1142   →   1200 = 18 minutes   I wait 1 hour 18 minutes
   1200   →   1300 = 1 hour

Remember there are only 60 minutes in 1 hour.

Solving numerical problems

Questions

1 Using a calculator work out 6.59×3.87, rounding your answer sensibly.

2 Keith has £65, he shares it equally between 6 people. How much does each receive?

3 Liam tries to work out the answer to $x^2 = 8$ by trial and improvement. What answer will he get to 1 decimal place? (Make up a table to help.)

4 The same brand of tuna fish is sold in two different sized tins. Which tin represents the better value for money?

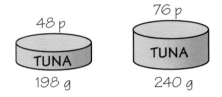

48 p

TUNA

198 g

76 p

TUNA

240 g

5 It is 9:34 p.m. Write this time as a 24 hour clock time.

6 The timetable shows the bus times from Amersham to Watford.

Amersham	0800	Every 30	1110	Every 60	1500
Rickmansworth	0822	minutes	1132	minutes	1522
Croxley Green	0831	until	1144	until	1531
West Watford	0847		1159		1547
Watford Junction	0903		1215		1603

(a) Jackie works in Croxley Green. If she travels on the 0822 bus from Rickmansworth, how long does her journey take?

(b) If Malcolm arrives at Amersham bus station at 1126, how long must he wait for the next bus to Watford Junction?

Functional relationships

Using letters

- **Algebra** uses letters to represent numbers.

Example

Emily plants a small vegetable garden. She plants potatoes, carrots and onions. m stands for the number of carrot seeds she has planted.

If she plants 5 more onion seeds than carrot seeds. How many onion seeds does she plant?

$m + 5$

This is known as an **expression**.

If she plants half as many onion seeds as carrot seeds, this is written as

$m \div 2$ which is usually written as $\dfrac{m}{2}$.

Remember that in algebra a division is usually written as a fraction, i.e. $x \div a = \dfrac{x}{a}$.

Example

Richard has p counters. David has three times as many counters. Write this as an expression:

David has $3 \times p$ counters.

- $3 \times p$ is written as $3p$ in algebra; the multiplication sign is missed out.

Substitution

- Replacing a letter with a number is called **substitution**. When substituting:

  write out the expression first then replace the letters with the values given,

  work out the value on your calculator. Use brackets keys where possible and pay attention to **order of operations**.

Examples

Using $a = 2$, $b = 4.1$, $c = -3$, $d = 5$, find the value of these expressions, giving your answer to 1 decimal place.

(a) $\dfrac{a + b}{2}$ (b) $\dfrac{a^2 + c^2}{d}$ (c) ab (d) $3d - ab$

Show each step in your working out.

Remember to show the substitution:

(a) $\dfrac{a + b}{2} = \dfrac{2 + 4.1}{2} = 3.05 = 3.1$ (1 d.p.)

> You may need to treat c^2 as $(-3)^2$ depending on your calculator.

(b) $\dfrac{a^2 + c^2}{d} = \dfrac{2^2 + (-3)^2}{5} = 2.6$

(c) $ab = 2 \times 4.1 = 8.2$

> ab means $a \times b$.

(d) $3d - ab = (3 \times 5) - (2 \times 4.1) = 6.8$.

Number patterns and sequences

A sequence is a list of numbers. There is usually a relationship between the numbers. Each value in the list is called a **term**.

- There are lots of different number patterns. When finding a missing number in the number pattern it is sensible to see what is happening in the gap.

Examples

The odd numbers have **a common difference** of two.

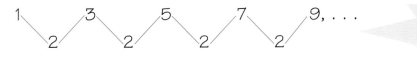

> The rule is add 2 each time.

The next term in this sequence is found by multiplying the previous term by 3.

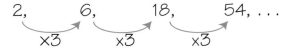

Common number patterns

These number patterns are common and need to be remembered.

1, 4, 9, 16, 25, ... Square numbers.

1, 8, 27, 64, 125, ... Cube numbers.

1, 3, 6, 10, 15, ... Triangular numbers.

1, 1, 2, 3, 5, 8, 13 ... Fibonacci sequence.

Finding the *n*th term of a linear sequence

- The *n*th term is often shown as U_n, e.g. the 12th term is U_{12}.

- For a linear sequence the *n*th term takes the form of $U_n = an + b$.

Example

Find the *n*th term of this sequence:

4, 7, 10, 13, 16.

- Look at the difference between the terms. If they are the same this gives the **multiple** or **a**.

- Adjust the rule by adding or taking away.

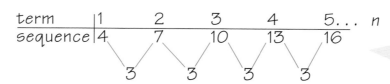

The gap or difference gives the value of a.

Check your rule with the second term to make sure it works.

The multiple is 3, i.e. 3*n*.

If *n* is 1, $3 \times 1 = 3$ but we need 4 so add 1.

*n*th term $U_n = 3n + 1$.

Coordinates

- Coordinates are used to locate the position of a point.

- When reading coordinates, read across first then up or down.

- Coordinates are always written with **brackets** and a **comma** in between, i.e. (2, 4)

- The horizontal axis is the **x** axis. The vertical axis is the **y** axis.

Examples

A has coordinates (2, 4)

B has coordinates (−1, 3)

C has coordinates (−2, −3)

D has coordinates (3, −1)

Remember to read across first then up or down!

> Make sure you write the brackets and comma.

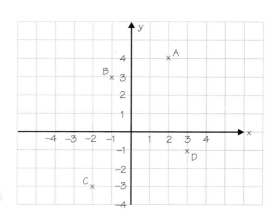

Function machines

Example

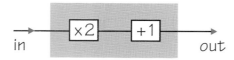

in   out

When the numbers are fed into this function machine, they are first multiplied by 2 and then added to 1.

If 1 is fed in, 3 comes out (i.e. $1 \times 2 + 1 = 3$)

If 2 is fed in, 5 comes out (i.e. $2 \times 2 + 1 = 5$)

If 3 is fed in, 7 comes out (i.e. $3 \times 2 + 1 = 7$)

If 4 is fed in, 9 comes out (i.e. $4 \times 2 + 1 = 9$)

This transformation can be illustrated with a **mapping diagram**, like this:

$$1 \rightarrow 3$$
$$2 \rightarrow 5$$
$$3 \rightarrow 7$$
$$4 \rightarrow 9$$

To describe the mapping, $x \rightarrow 2x + 1$ is written.
This is read   'x becomes 2x + 1'.

Graph drawing

- Coordinates are used to draw graphs.

- Before a graph can be drawn the coordinates need to be worked out.

Graphs of the form $y = mx + c$

These are straight line (linear) graphs.

The general equation of a straight line graph is $y = mx + c$.

m is the **gradient** (steepness) of the line.

c is the **intercept** on the y axis, that is where the graph cuts the y axis.

Parallel lines have the **same gradient**.

Example

Draw the graphs of $y = 2x$, $y = -2x$, $y = 3x$ and $y = x - 2$ on the same axes.

- Work out coordinates for each graph.

> Putting the coordinates in a table makes it easier.

If your line is not straight, go back and check your coordinates.

$y = 2x$

x	-2	-1	0	1	2
y	-4	-2	0	2	4

$y = -2x$

x	-2	-1	0	1	2
y	4	2	0	-2	-4

$y = 3x$

x	-2	-1	0	1	2
y	-6	-3	0	3	6

$y = x - 2$

x	-2	-1	0	1	2
y	-4	-3	-2	-1	0

- Plot each set of coordinates and join up the points with a straight line.

- Label each of the graphs.

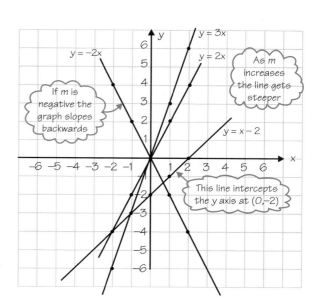

If m is negative the graph slopes backwards

As m increases the line gets steeper

This line intercepts the y axis at (0,-2)

Graphs of the form y = a, x = b

Example

Draw the line $y = 3$.

Example

Draw the line $x = 2$.

$y = a$ is a **horizontal** line with every y coordinate equal to a.
$x = b$ is a **vertical** line with every x coordinate equal to b.

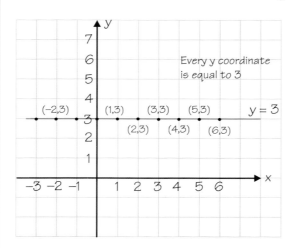

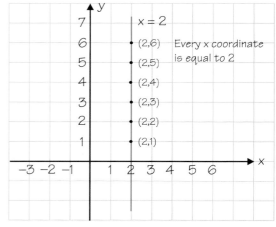

Graphs of the form y = x² + a

- These are curved graphs.

Example

Draw the graph of $y = x^2 - 2$.

x	−3	−2	−1	0	1	2	3
y	7	2	−1	−2	−1	2	7

> Use a calculator to help work out the coordinates.

- Work out the y coordinates for each point.

- Remember that x^2 means x times x.

- Just replace x in the equation with each coordinate, i.e.
  $x = -3$ so $y = (-3)^2 - 2 = 7$.

> Try and join the points with a smooth curve.

- The table represents the coordinates of the graph. The coordinates can now be plotted to form the graph.

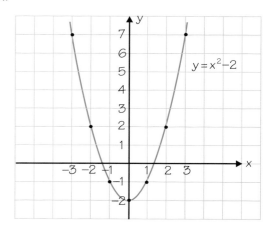

- Join up the points with a smooth curve and label the graph.

Using linear graphs

- Linear graphs are often used to show relationships.

Examples

The graph shows the charges made by a van hire firm.

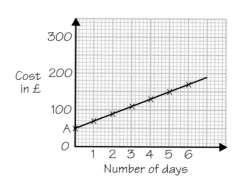

- Point A shows how much was charged for hiring the van, i.e. £50.

- The gradient shows that £20 was then charged per day. Hence for 5 days' hire, the van cost £50 + 20 × 5 = £150.

Conversion graphs

- These are used to convert one measurement into another measurement.

When reading off the graph draw on lines to show how you obtained your answers.

Example

£1 = 200 pesetas.

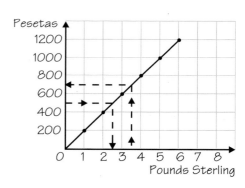

- To change £3.50 into pesetas read up to the line and then across, i.e. 700 pesetas.

- To change 500 pesetas read across to the line and then read down, i.e. £2.50.

Functional relationships

Questions

1 Write these expressions as simply as possible.

(a) 6 more than n (b) 4 less than p (c) 6 more than 3 lots of y

(d) h divided by 7   (e) 5 less than n divided by p

2 If $a = 3$, $b = 2.1$, $c = -4$, work out the answer to these expressions giving your answer to 1 d.p.

(a) $3a + 2b$ (b) $5c - 2a$ (c) abc

3 Find the nth term of this sequence
2, 6, 10, 14, . . .

4 Find the nth term of this sequence
5, 8, 11, 14, 17, . . .

5 What are the coordinates of the
points A, B, C, D, E and F?

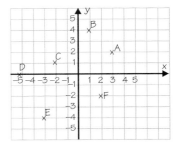

6 The graph of $y = x - 1$ is drawn on the
graph opposite. Draw the following
graphs on the same axes.

(a) $y = 2x$

(b) $y = 4x$

(c) What do you notice about the
graphs of $y = 2x$ and $y = 4x$?

(d) Without working out any
coordinates draw the graph of
$y = x - 2$.

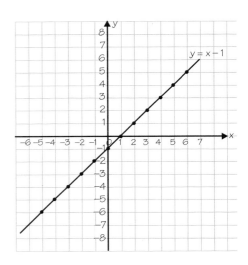

Equations and formulae

Algebraic conventions

- There are several rules to follow when writing algebra.

  $a + a + a + a = 4a$

  $b \times b = b^2$ **not** $2b$

  $b \times b \times b = b^3$ **not** $3b$

  $n \times n \times 3 = 3n^2$ **not** $(3n)^2$

  $a \times 3 \times c = 3ac$

  Put the number first and then the letters in alphabetical order; leave out the multiplication sign.

- When dividing, i.e. $a \div 3$, this is usually written as a fraction, i.e. $\dfrac{a}{3}$.

Writing simple formulae

$n + 4$ is an expression.

$y = n + 4$ is a formula, since it has an = sign in it.

Example

A bag of sweets costs 20p. Erin buys some sweets. How much do

(a) 6 bags cost? (b) 10 bags cost? (c) x bags cost?

(a) $20 \times 6 = 120$ pence.

(b) $20 \times 10 = 200$ pence.

(c) $20 \times x = 20x$ pence.

x can take any value.

In words the above rule can be written as:
Cost of sweets = 20 × number of bags.

This is a **formula** for working out the cost of any number of bags of sweets. If C represents the cost and b represents the number of bags then:

$C = 20 \times b$

i.e. $C = 20b$, this formula is in **symbol form**.

Example

The diagrams show some black and white tiles.

number
pattern 1

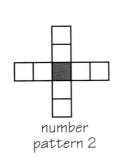

number
pattern 2

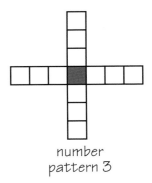

number
pattern 3

(a) How many white tiles will there be in pattern number 4?

Drawing the diagram:

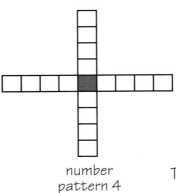

number
pattern 4

There are 16 white tiles.

(b) Write down the formula for finding the number of tiles in pattern number n.

Number of tiles = $4 \times n + 1$
= $4n + 1$.

Make sure an = sign is in the formula.

The 4n is the 4 lots of white tiles. The +1 is the black tile in the middle.

(c) How many tiles will be used in pattern number 12?

$n = 12$, i.e. number of tiles = $4 \times 12 + 1$
= $48 + 1$
= 49.

Just substitute the value of n into the formula.

Substituting values into formulae

This is the same as substituting values into expressions. Simply replace the letters with the values.

Example

$P = 3 \times (a + b)$. Work out the value of P if $a = 3.1$ and $b = 5$.

Show full working out.

$$P = 3 \times (3.1 + 5)$$
$$= 3 \times (8.1)$$
$$= 24.3$$

Work out the brackets first.

Example

The formula $F = 1.8C + 32$ is used to change temperature in degrees centigrade (C) to temperatures in degrees Fahrenheit (F).
If $C = 20$, work out the value of F.

Work this out carefully on your calculator.

$$F = 1.8C + 32$$
$$= 1.8 \times 20 + 32$$
$$= 68$$

Substitute $C = 20$ into the formula. Note $1.8C$ means $1.8 \times C$

Collecting like terms

- Expressions can be simplified by collecting like terms.

- Only collect the terms if the letters and powers are identical.

Examples

$3p + 2p = 5p$.

$6a + 2c$ cannot be simplified, since there are no like terms.

$5n + 2n - 6n = n$

Note that n means $1n$.

Remember to put the sign between, i.e. $5a + 2b$ **NOT** $5a \ 2b$.

$2a + 4b + 3a - 2b = 5a + 2b$.

This minus sign is part of the term $2b$.

Add the a's then the b's.

$5xy + 2yx = 7xy$ since xy is the same as yx.

Multiplying letters and numbers

- Algebraic expressions are often simplified by multiplying them together, i.e. $5a \times 2b = 10ab$.

- When multiplying expressions, multiply the numbers together then the letters together.

Examples

Simplify these expressions:

Multiply the letters

(a) $3a \times 4b = 3 \times 4 \times a \times b = 12ab$.

Multiply the numbers

(b) $5a \times 3b \times 2c = 5 \times 3 \times 2 \times a \times b \times c = 30abc$.

Remember $a \times a = a^2$.

(c) $2a \times 3a = 2 \times 3 \times a \times a = 6a^2$.

Multiplying out brackets

- This helps to simplify algebraic expressions.

- Multiply everything inside the brackets by everything outside the brackets.

Examples

*This is known as **expanding** brackets.*

$2(a + b) = 2a + 2b$.

$3(x - 2) = 3x - 6$.

The multiplication sign is not shown here.

Remember $r \times r = r^2$.

$a(b + d) = ab + ad$.

$r(3r - 2s) = 3r^2 - 2rs$

If the term outside the brackets is **negative**, all of the signs of the terms inside the brackets are **changed** when multiplying out.

Remember that $-(a + b)$ means $-1 \times (a + b)$.

Examples

$-2(a + b) = -2a - 2b$

$-a(a - b) = -a^2 + ab$

To simplify expressions, expand the brackets first then collect like terms.

Example

Expand and simplify:

$3(a + 1) + 2(a + b)$ Multiply out brackets.

$3a + 3 + 2a + 2b$ Collect like terms.
$= 5a + 2b + 3.$

Inequalities

These are expressions, where one side is **not equal** to the other.

< 'is less than'   ≤ 'is less than or equal to'

> 'is greater than'   ≥ 'is greater than or equal to'

Examples

$-6 < 5$ $5 > 2$

Linear equations

- An equation involves an unknown value which has to be worked out.
- The balance method is usually used, that is whatever is done to one side of an equation must be done to the other.

Examples

Solve the following:

Show all working out and do the calculation step by step.

(a) $n - 4 = 6$

$n = 6 + 4$ Add 4 to both sides.

$n = 10$

(b) $n + 2 = 8$

$n = 8 - 2$ Subtract 2 from both sides.

$n = 6$

(c) $5n = 20$

$n = \dfrac{20}{5}$

$n = 4$

Divide both sides by 5.

(d) $\dfrac{n}{3} = 2$

$n = 2 \times 3$

$n = 6$

Multiply both sides by 3.

(e) $5n + 1 = 11$

$5n = 11 - 1$

$5n = 10$

$n = \dfrac{10}{5} = 2.$

Subtract 1 from both sides.

Divide both sides by 5.

(f) $\dfrac{n}{3} + 1 = 4$

$\dfrac{n}{3} = 4 - 1$

$\dfrac{n}{3} = 3$

$n = 3 \times 3$

$n = 9.$

Multiply both sides by 3

The answers are not always whole numbers, they can be fractions, decimals and negative values as well.

(g) $5(2x - 1) = 10$

$10x - 5 = 10$

$10x = 10 + 5$

$10x = 15$

$x = \dfrac{15}{10} = 1.5.$

Multiply brackets out first.

(h) $7x - 2 = 2x + 13$

$7x - 2 - 2x = 13$

$5x = 13 + 2$

$5x = 15$

$x = \dfrac{15}{5} = 3.$

Subtract 2x from both sides. Add 2 to both sides.

(i) $4(2n + 5) = 3(n + 10)$

$8n + 20 = 3n + 30$

$8n + 20 - 3n = 30$

$5n = 30 - 20$

$5n = 10$

$n = \dfrac{10}{5} = 2.$

Multiply brackets out first.

Using equations to solve problems

Example

Class 9A were playing a number game. Saima said "Multiplying my number by 5 and adding 8 gives the same answer as subtracting my number from 20."

(a) Call Saima's number y and form an equation.

$$5y + 8 = 20 - y$$

(b) Solve the equation to work out Saima's number:

$$5y + 8 = 20 - y$$

$$5y + 8 + y = 20$$

$$6y = 20 - 8$$

$$6y = 12$$

$$y = \frac{12}{6} = 2.$$ Saima's number is 2.

Check at the end that $y = 2$ works in the equation.

Equations and formulae

Questions

1

pattern 1   pattern 2   pattern 3

The diagram shows some patterns made up with sticks. If P represents the pattern number and S represents the number of sticks. Write down a formula connecting S and P.

2 Simplify these expressions:

(a) $5a + 2a + 3a$

(b) $6a - 2b + 5b$

(c) $3xy + 2yx$

(d) $5a \times 2b$

(e) $3a \times 4a$

(f) $6a + 2b - 2b + b$

3 A shape has the lengths as shown in the diagram. Write down an expression for the perimeter of the shape.

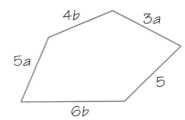

4 Some cards have the following expressions written on them:

A   B   C   D

| $2a + 8$ | $2a + 4$ | $4a + 8$ | $4a + 2$ |

Which card is the same as $4(a + 2)$?

5 Solve the following equations:

(a) $5a + 10 = 15$

(b) $\frac{n}{5} - 1 = 6$

(c) $5n + 1 = 11$

(d) $6n + 2 = 4n + 8$

(e) $6(n + 2) = 5n + 7$

(f) $2(n - 1) = 3(n + 4)$

6 If $P = 2 \times (L + W)$ find P if L = 3.1 and W = 1.4.

7 If $Y = 20n + 5$ find Y if $n = 5$.

Shape, space and measure

Symmetry

Reflective symmetry

Examiner's tips and your notes

If asked to complete a shape to make it symmetrical use tracing paper to help.

- Both sides of a shape are symmetrical when a mirror line is drawn across it. The mirror line is known as the **line** or **axis of symmetry**.

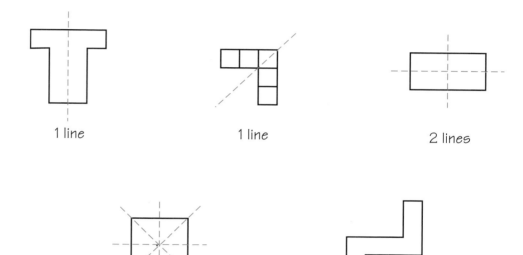

| 1 line | 1 line | 2 lines |

4 lines   no lines

Example

Half a reflected shape is shown here. The dashed line is a line of symmetry. Copy and complete the shape.

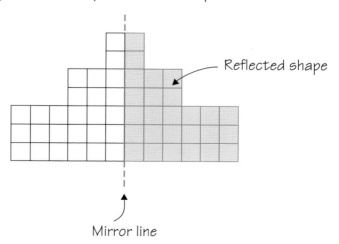

Reflected shape

Mirror line

Rotational symmetry

- A 2D (two-dimensional) shape has rotational symmetry, if when it is turned, it looks exactly the same. The **order of rotational symmetry** is the number of times the shape turns and looks the same.

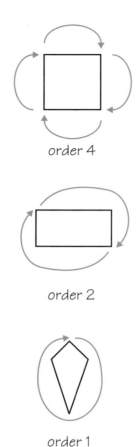

order 4

order 2

order 1

For the kite the shape has 1 position. It is said to have **rotational symmetry of order 1** or **no** rotational symmetry.

Plane symmetry

This is symmetry in 3D (three-dimensional) solids only.

A 3D shape has a plane of symmetry if the plane divides the shape into two halves, and one half is the exact mirror image of the other.

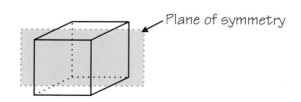

Plane of symmetry

2D shapes

Triangles

There are several types of triangles.

Right angled

Has a 90°
angle.

Equilateral

3 sides equal.
3 angles equal.

Isosceles

2 sides equal.
Base angles equal.

Scalene

No sides or
angles the same.

Quadrilaterals

You need to be able to sketch these shapes and know their symmetrical properties.

These are four-sided shapes.

Square

4 lines of symmetry.
Rotational symmetry of order 4.

Rectangle

2 lines of symmetry.
Rotational symmetry of order 2

47

Parallelogram

No lines of symmetry.
Rotational symmetry of order 2.

Rhombus

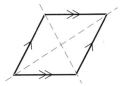

2 lines of symmetry.
Rotational symmetry of order 2.

Kite

1 line of symmetry.
No rotational symmetry.

Trapezium

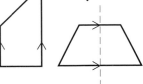

Isosceles trapezium:
1 line of symmetry.
No rotational symmetry.

Parallel lines are lines that remain the same distance apart, i.e. they never meet.

Polygons

These are 2D shapes with **straight** sides. **Regular polygons** are shapes with all sides and angles equal.

Number of sides	Name of polygon
3	Triangle
4	Quadrilateral
5	Pentagon
6	Hexagon
7	Heptagon
8	Octagon

3D shapes

Cube   **Cuboid**

Sphere

Cylinder   **Cone**

A prism is a solid that can be cut into slices which are all the same shape.

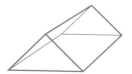

Triangular prism   **Square-based pyramid**

Drawing shapes

Nets of solids

The net of a 3D shape is a 2D shape which is folded to make the 3D shape.

When making the shape remember to put tabs on to stick together.

Examples

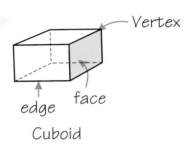

Cuboid

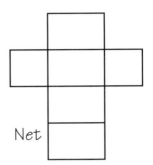

Net

When asked to draw an accurate net, you must measure carefully.

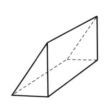

Triangular prism

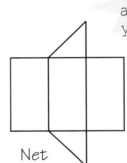

Net

Plans and elevations

A **plan** is what is seen if a 3D shape is looked down on from above.

An **elevation** is seen if the 3D shape is looked at from the side or front.

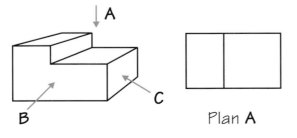

Plan **A**

Front elevation **B**

Side elevation **C**

Angles

An **acute** angle is between 0° and 90°.

An **obtuse** angle is between 90° and 180°.

A **reflex** angle is between 180° and 360°.

A **right angle** is 90°.

Measuring angles using a protractor

A protractor is used to measure the size of an angle.

When measuring angles count the degree lines carefully and always double check.

Beware, make sure you put the 0° line at the start position and read from the correct scale.

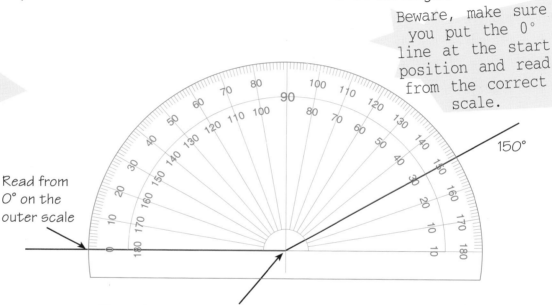

Read from 0° on the outer scale

150°

Place the cross at the point of the angle you are measuring

For the above angle measure on the outer scale since you must start from 0°.

Angle facts

You must remember these angle facts as you will need to apply them to questions.

Angles on a **straight line** add up to **180°**
$a + b + c = 180°$.

Angles at a **point** add up to **360°**
$a + b + c = 360°$.

Angles in a **triangle** add up to **180°**

$a + b + c = 180°$.

Angles in a **quadrilateral** add up to **360°**

$a + b + c + d = 360°$.

Vertically opposite angles are equal.

$a = b$, $c = d$.

$a + c = b + d = 180°$

An **exterior angle** of a triangle equals the sum of the two opposite **interior angles**.

$a + b = c$.

Angles in parallel lines

Alternate (z) angles are **equal**.

Corresponding angles are **equal**.

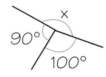

Supplementary angles add up to **180°**

$c + d = 180°$.

Examples

Find the angles labelled by letters:

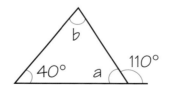

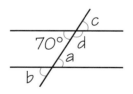

$x + 90° + 100°$
$= 360°$
$x = 360° - 190°$
$x = 170°$.

$a + 110° = 180°$
$a = 70°$.
$70° + 40° + b$
$\quad = 180°$
$b = 180° - 110°$
$b = 70°$.

$a = 70°$ (alternate).
$b = 70°$ (corresponding).
$c = 70°$ (corresponding to a).
$d = 180 - 70 = 110°$ (angles on a straight line).

Show full working out.

Reading angles

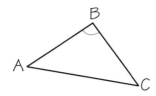

When asked to find ABC or ∠ABC or AB̂C, find the angle shown by the **middle letter**, in this case B.

Angles in polygons

There are two types of angles in a polygon: **interior** (inside) and **exterior** (outside).

For a regular polygon with n sides:

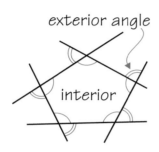

- Sum of exterior angles = 360°.

  So exterior angle = $\dfrac{360°}{n}$

- Interior angle + exterior angle = 180°.

- Sum of interior angles = $(n - 2) \times 180°$.

Example

Calculate the interior and exterior angle of a regular pentagon.

A pentagon has 5 sides, i.e. $n = 5$.

Exterior angle = $\dfrac{360}{5}$ = 72°.

Interior angle + exterior angle = 180°.

Interior angle = 180° − 72°

$\qquad\qquad\quad$ = 108°.

Properties of shapes

Questions

1 The dotted lines are the lines of symmetry. Complete the shape so that it is symmetrical.

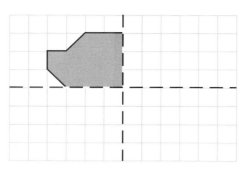

2 What is the name of a six-sided polygon?

3 Draw an accurate net of this 3D shape.

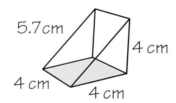

4 Find the size of the angles labelled by letters:

(a)

(b)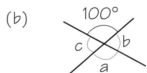

(c)

(d)

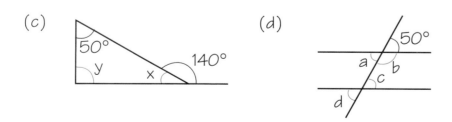

5 Find the size of (a) an exterior (b) an interior angle of a regular hexagon.

Properties of position, movement and transformation

Tessellations

- A tessellation is a pattern of 2D shapes which fit together without leaving any gaps.

- For shapes to tessellate, the angles at each point must add up to 360°.

Example

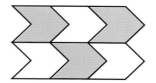

Compass directions

The diagram shows the points of the compass.

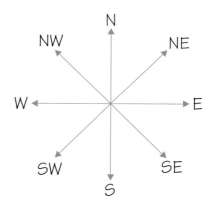

Example

If Paulo is facing East and turns clockwise through an angle of 270°. What direction will he now be facing?

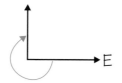

Remember clockwise is this direction.

Paulo will now be facing North.

Bearings

- Bearings give a direction in degrees.

- Bearings are always measured from the **North** in a **clockwise** direction. They must have **3 figures**.

Examples

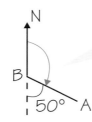

Measure from the North line at B.

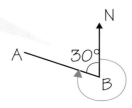

The word **'from'** is very important. It tells you where to put the North line and measure from.

Bearing of A **from** B
= 180° − 50° = 130°.

Bearing of A **from** B
= 360° − 30° = 330°.

When finding the **back bearing** (the bearing of B **from** A above)

- draw a North line at A

- use the properties of parallel lines, since both North lines are parallel.

Examples

Look for alternate (Z) or corresponding angles.

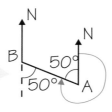

Measure from the North line at A.

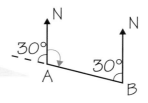

Bearing of B from A
= 360° − 50°
= 310°.

Bearing of B from A
= 180° − 30°
= 150°.

Transformations

- A **transformation** changes the **position** or **size** of a shape.

Rotations

Notice that the rotated shapes are congruent, that is they are exactly the same size and shape.

- Rotations turn a figure through an angle about some fixed point. This fixed point is called the **centre of rotation.**

- The size or shape of the figure is not changed.

Example

This is a 90° rotation about O, in a clockwise direction (also known as a $\frac{1}{4}$ turn clockwise).

O (centre of rotation)

Enlargements

- These change the size but not the shape of an object.

- The **centre of enlargement** is the point from which the enlargement takes place.

- The **scale factor** indicates how many times the length of the original figure has changed size.

- If the scale factor is **greater than 1**, the shape becomes **bigger**.

Example

Enlarge shape ABCDEF by a scale factor of 2, centre = (0, 0). Call it A′ B′ C′ D′ E′ F′.

If asked to describe an enlargement, state the centre of enlargement and the scale factor.

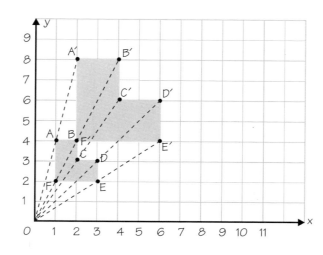

Notice that each side of the enlargement is twice the size of the original.

OA′ = 2OA.

Reflections

Reflections create an image of an object on the other side of a mirror line. The mirror line is known as an **axis of reflection**. The size or shape of the figure is not changed.

Example

Reflect triangle ABC in the mirror line.

Plot the image points first. They are the same distance from the mirror as the object. Join up the image points.

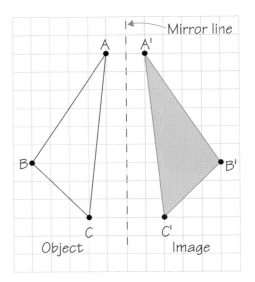

LOGO

- This is a computer program which is used to draw shapes.

- Transformations can take place using LOGO.

Example

Shape Y is an equilateral triangle. The instructions to draw shape Y are:

FORWARD 4.

TURN RIGHT 120°.

FORWARD 4.

TURN RIGHT 120°.

FORWARD 4.

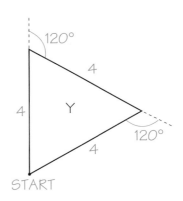

Constructions

The perpendicular bisector of a line

- Draw a line XY.

- Draw two arcs, with the compasses using X as the centre. The compasses must be set at a radius greater than half the distance of XY.

- Draw two more arcs with Y as the centre (keep the compasses the same distance apart as before).

- Join the two points where the arcs cross.

- AB is the **perpendicular bisector** of XY.

- N is the **midpoint** of XY.

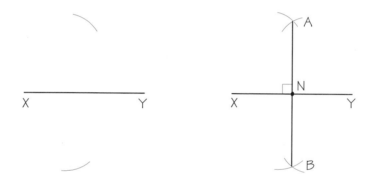

Bisecting an angle

- Draw two lines XY and YZ to meet at an angle.

- Using compasses, place the point at Y and draw the two arcs on XY and YZ.

- Place the compass points at the two arcs on XY and YZ and draw arcs to cross at N. Join Y to N.

YN is the **bisector** of angle XYZ.

Practise by bisecting your own angles.

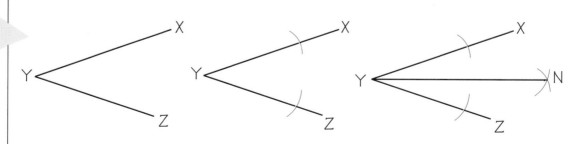

Scale drawings

Scale drawings are very useful for measuring lengths which cannot be measured directly.

Example

Here is a rough sketch of a sector of a circle. Using a scale of 1 cm to 2 m draw an accurate drawing of the sector.

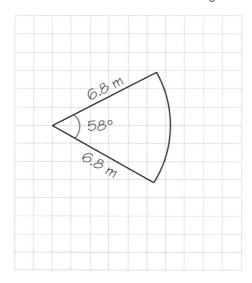

A scale of 1 cm to 2 m means that 6.8 m is 6.8 ÷ 2 = 3.4 cm on the diagram.

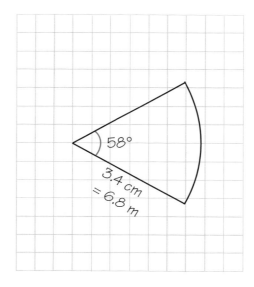

Properties of position, movement and transformation

Questions

1 What are the bearings of X from Y in the following:

(a)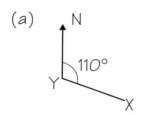

(b)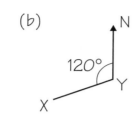

(c)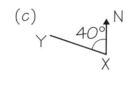

2 Enlarge shape P by a scale factor of 2, call it A

Centre of enlargement is at (0, 0).

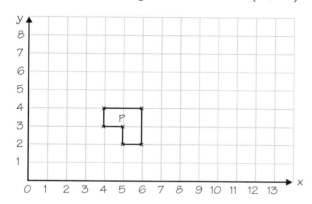

3 Shape A is a rectangle.

Complete the LOGO commands for drawing
the rectangle:

FORWARD 2.

TURN RIGHT 90°.

FORWARD 5.

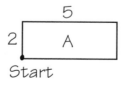

4 Bisect this angle:

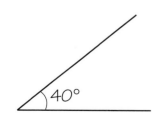

Measures

Metric units

Length	Weight	Capacity
10 mm = 1 cm	1000 mg = 1 g	1000 ml = 1 l
100 cm = 1 m	1000 g = 1 kg	100 cl = 1 l
1000 m = 1 km	1000 kg = 1 tonne	1000 cm³ = 1 l

Converting units

- If changing from **small** units to **large** units (e.g. g to kg) **divide**.
- If changing from **large** units to **small** units (e.g. km to m) **multiply**.

Examples

$500 \text{ cm} = 5 \text{ m} (\div 100)$. $5\,l = 500\,cl \ (\times 100)$.

$3500 \text{ g} = 3.5 \text{ kg} (\div 1000)$. $25 \text{ cm} = 250 \text{ mm} (\times 10)$.

Imperial units

Length	Weight	Capacity
1 foot = 12 inches	1 stone = 14 pounds (lb)	20 fluid oz = 1 pint
1 yard = 3 feet	1 pound = 16 ounces (oz)	8 pints = 1 gallon

Comparisons between metric and imperial units

Length	Weight	Capacity
2.5 cm ≈ 1 inch	25 g ≈ 1 ounce	1 litre ≈ $1\frac{3}{4}$ pints
30 cm ≈ 1 foot	1 kg ≈ 2.2 pounds	4.5 litres ≈ 1 gallon
1 m ≈ 39 inches		
8 km ≈ 5 miles		

Example

Change 8 inches into cm.

1 inch ≈ 2.5 cm.

8 inches = 8 × 2.5 = 20 cm.

Reading scales

Decimals are usually used when reading off scales. Measuring jugs, rulers, weighing scales are all examples of scales which have decimals.

Examples

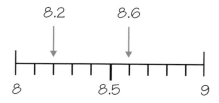 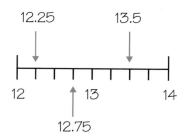

There are 10 spaces between the 8 and the 9. Each space is 0.1.

There are 5 spaces between the 6 and the 7. Each space is 0.2.

There are 4 spaces between the 12 and 13. Each space is 0.25.

Areas and volumes

Perimeter – this is the distance around the outside edge of a shape.

Area – this is the amount of space a 2D shape covers. Common units of area are mm², cm², m², etc.

Volume – this is the amount of space a 3D shape occupies. Common units of volume are mm³, cm³, m³, etc.

Perimeter of 2D shapes

Example

Find the perimeter of this shape:

Perimeter = 4 + 5 + 3 + 2.7 + 2.7
= 17.4 cm

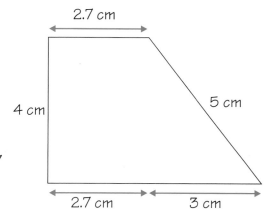

Estimating areas of irregular shapes

Areas of irregular shapes can be estimated by counting the squares the shape covers.

Example

- Label the squares as you count them.
- Try to match up parts of squares to make a whole one.

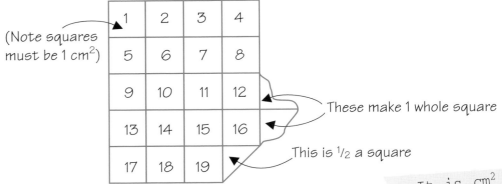

(Note squares must be 1 cm^2)

These make 1 whole square

This is ½ a square

The shape has an area of $20\frac{1}{2}$ cm^2

It is cm^2 because each square is 1cm^2.

Areas of quadrilaterals and triangles

Remember perpendicular height just means the height which is 90° to the base.

Area of a rectangle

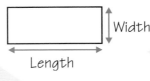

Width

Length

Write the formulae using letters. It's quicker.

Area = Length × Width.

$A = L \times W.$

Area of a parallelogram

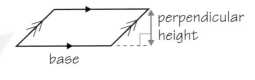

perpendicular height

base

Area = Base × Perpendicular height.

$A = b \times h.$

Area of a triangle

perpendicular height

base

$A = \frac{1}{2} \times$ Base × Perpendicular height.

$A = \frac{1}{2} \times b \times h.$

Area of a trapezium

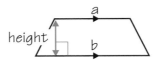

height

a

b

$A = \frac{1}{2} \times$ (Sum of parallel sides) × Perpendicular height.

$A = \frac{1}{2} \times (a + b) \times h.$

Examples

Find the area of the following shapes.

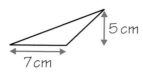

$A = \frac{1}{2} \times b \times h.$

$A = \frac{1}{2} \times 7 \times 5 = 17.5$ cm².

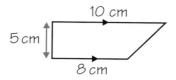

$A = \frac{1}{2} \times (a + b) \times h.$

$A = \frac{1}{2} \times (10 + 8) \times 5 = 45$ cm².

Circumference and area of a circle

circumference

Circumference = π × diameter $C = \pi \times d$

               = 2 × π × radius $= 2 \times \pi \times r$

Area   = π × (radius)² $A = \pi \times r^2$

> Remember r^2 means $r \times r$.

Example

> Remember that the circumference of a circle is the distance around the outside edge.

Mohammed's bicycle wheel has a diameter of 60 cm. Work out the circumference of the wheel, using π = 3.14.

$C = \pi \times d$

$C = 3.14 \times 60$

$C = 188.4$ cm

> Use π = 3.14 or the value of π on your calculator, if you are not told in the question.

If Mohammed travels a distance of 50 m on the bicycle, how many times does his wheel turn around?

Change 50 m into cm first, i.e. 50 × 100 = 5000 cm

Distance ÷ Circumference = No. of turns.

> Check that the answer is sensible.

$\dfrac{5000}{188.4} = 26.5$ times.

> Always check the units are the same before starting a question.

The wheel must turn 27 times to go a distance of 50 m.

Example

Find the area of a circular rose garden, which has a diameter of 2.6 m. Use π = 3.142.

Diameter = 2.6 m

Radius = 2.6 ÷ 2 = 1.3 m.

Area = π × r²

       = 3.142 × 1.3².   Remember 1.3² means 1.3 × 1.3.

       = 5.3 m² (1 d.p.).

Volumes of 3D shapes

Estimating voumes of 3D shapes

The volume of a 3D shape can be found by counting the number of 1 cm³ cubes.

Example

The volume of this shape is 24 cm³

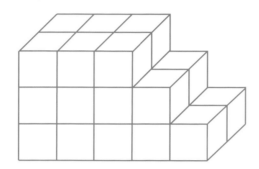

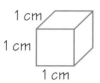

This cube has a volume of 1 cm³ (1 cubic centimetre)

1 cm
1 cm
1 cm

Volume of a cuboid

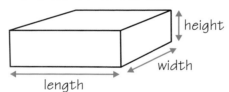

height
width
length

Volume =
Length × Width × Height

$$V = l \times w \times h.$$

Volume of a prism

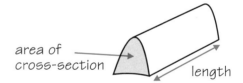

area of cross-section
length

Volume =
Area of cross-section × Length

$$V = a \times l.$$

A prism is any solid which can be cut into slices, which are all the same shape. This is called having a **uniform cross-section.**

Example

A door wedge is in the shape of a trapezium. Work out the volume of the door wedge.

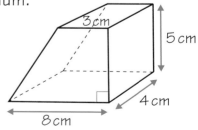

3 cm
5 cm
4 cm
8 cm

Area of cross-section:

$$A = \frac{(a + b) \times h}{2}$$

$$\frac{(3 + 8) \times 5}{2} = 27.5 \text{ cm}^2$$

Volume = 27.5 × 4 = 110 cm³.

Substitute values in carefully and show full working out.

Remember to find the volume, multiply the area of cross-section by the length.

Measures
Questions

1 Change 6200 g into kg.

2 Change 4.2 cm into mm.

3 Change 6 litres into pints.

4 What do the pointers on the scales represent?

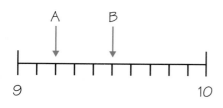 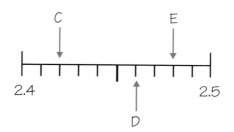 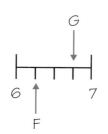

5 Work out the area of the following shapes, giving your answer to 1 d.p.

(a)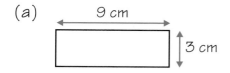

(b)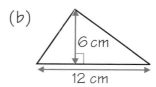

(c)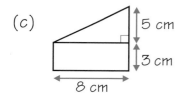

(d)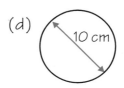

6 Work out the volume of these 3D shapes, giving your answer to 1 d.p.

(a)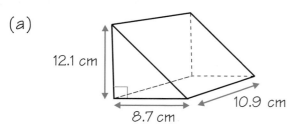

(b)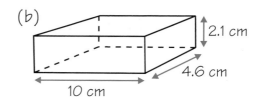

7 Work out the circumference of a circle with radius of 4.9 cm. Use π = 3.14.

Handling data

Types of data

- **Discrete data** – each category is separate. It is often found by counting. Examples include the number of red cars in a car park.

- **Continuous data** – here the values change from one category to the next. Such data is often found by measuring. Examples include the height and shoe size of year 8 pupils.

Surveys and questionnaires

- Data can be collected by carrying out **surveys** using **questionnaires**.

- A **hypothesis** is a prediction which can be tested and usually gives a purpose to the survey, i.e. most staff at the school have a red car.

- An **observation sheet** is used to collect data. They must be clear and easy to use.

Example

Colour of staff cars

Colour	Tally	Frequency
red		
blue		
white		
green		
black		
others		

Questionnaires

When designing questionnaires:

- Keep the questionnaire short.

- Give instructions on how to fill it in.

Word any questions you write very carefully.

- Ask questions which cover the purpose of your survey.

- Do not ask for information which is not needed, e.g. name.

- Make sure that your opinion is not evident, e.g. do you agree that 'Neighbours' is better than 'Home and Away'?

- Allow for any possible outcomes:

Example

How much do you spend on magazines each week?

Under £1 ☐   £1–£2 ☐   £2.01–£3 ☐   over £3 ☐

Collecting information

- Data which has been collected can be sorted by putting it into a table called a **tally chart** or **frequency table**.

- The tally chart shows the frequency of each item (how often the item occurs).

- A tally is just a line I, which when grouped into fives make them easier to count. The fifth one forms a gate, i.e. IIII.

Grouping data

If the data covers a large range of results, it is usual to group the data into **class intervals**, where each class interval is the same width. For continuous data the class intervals are often written using **inequalities**.

Example

The heights in cm of 30 pupils were:

To help: cross off the data as you put it in the table.

137	142	139	120	152
126	149	147	138	135
135	132	127	154	150
138	144	149	150	122
140	142	138	141	149
127	125	141	140	135

Height (cm)	Tally	Frequency
120 ≤ h <125	II	2
125 ≤ h <130	IIII	4
130 ≤ h <135	I	1
135 ≤ h <140	IIII III	8
140 ≤ h <145	HHT II	7
145 ≤ h <150	IIII	4
150 ≤ h <155	IIII	4
	Total	30

Always check the total at the end to make sure all data is included.

- The data has been grouped into class intervals of 5.

- Choose sensible groupings of 2, 5 or 10.

- Check that all data has been included.

$120 \le h < 125$ means that the heights are all between 120 and 125 cm.

$120 \le h$ means that the height can be equal to 120 cm.

$h < 125$ means that the height cannot be equal to 125 cm. It would be in the next group.

Representing information

Pie charts

- These are circles split up into sections. Each section represents a certain number of items.

Calculating angles for a pie chart

- Find the total for the items listed.

- Find the fraction of the total for each item.

- Multiply the fraction by 360° to find the angle.

Remember there are 360° at the centre of the circle.

Example

The favourite sports of 24 students in year 9.

Sport	Frequency
Football	9
Swimming	5
Netball	3
Hockey	7

Finding the angle

9 out of 24 like football, i.e. $\dfrac{9}{24} \times 360° = 135°$.

fraction — multiply by 360°.

Key in on the calculator:

| 9 | ÷ | 24 | × | 360 | = |

Football $= \dfrac{9}{24} \times 360° = 135°$

Swimming $= \dfrac{5}{24} \times 360° = 75°$

Netball $= \dfrac{3}{24} \times 360° = 45°$

Hockey $= \dfrac{7}{24} \times 360° = 105°$

Total $= 360°$

Check that your angles add up to 360°.

Measure the angles carefully with a protractor.

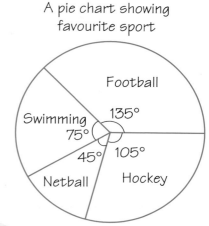

A pie chart showing favourite sport

Interpreting pie charts

The pie chart shows how some students travel to school.

There are 18 students in total.

How many travel by (a) Car?

(b) Bus?

(c) Walk?

$360° = 18$ students

$1° = \dfrac{18}{360°} = 0.05$ (work out 1°)

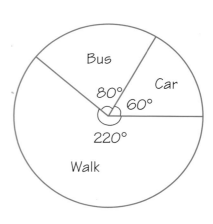

Check your answers sound sensible.

Car = 60° × 0.05 = 3 students.

Bus = 80° × 0.05 = 4 students.

Walk = 220° × 0.05 = 11 students.

Line graphs

These are a set of points joined by a line. Line graphs can be used to show **continuous data**.

Example

Year	1989	1990	1991	1992	1993	1994	1995	1996
Number of cars sold	420	530	480	560	590	620	490	440

The **middle values** (for example point Y) have no meaning. Point Y does not mean that halfway between 1994 and 1995 550 cars were sold.

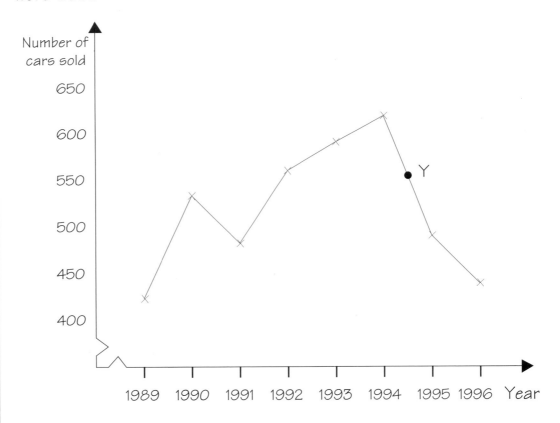

Frequency diagrams

- These are drawn to illustrate **continuous data**.

- They are similar to bar charts except there are no gaps between the bars.

- The data must be grouped into equal class intervals if the length of the bar is used to represent the frequency.

Example

The heights of 30 pupils are grouped as shown in the table.

Height (cm)	Frequency
$120 \leq h < 125$	2
$125 \leq h < 130$	4
$130 \leq h < 135$	1
$135 \leq h < 140$	8
$140 \leq h < 145$	7
$145 \leq h < 150$	4
$150 \leq h < 155$	4
	30

Check that you've labelled the axes and written a title.

- The axes do not need to start at zero.

- Do not leave a gap between the bars.

- Label the axes and write a title.

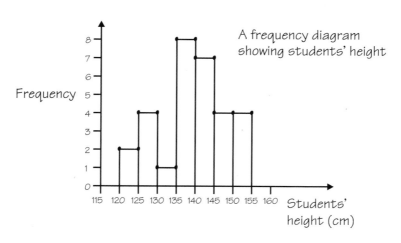

A frequency diagram showing students' height

Frequency polygons

- These are used to join the midpoints of the class intervals for grouped or continuous data.
- To draw the frequency polygon put a cross on the middle of the bar and join the crosses up with a ruler.
- Draw a line down from the middle of the first and last bar to the x axis.

Example

Consider the frequency diagram of the students' height.

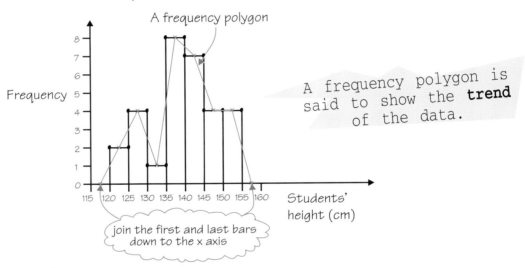

A frequency polygon is said to show the **trend** of the data.

join the first and last bars down to the x axis

Scatter diagrams

- A scatter diagram (scattergraph) is used to show two sets of data at the same time.
- It is used to show the connection (**correlation**) between two sets of data. There are three types of correlation: **positive**, **negative** or **zero**.

In the SATs examination, you must be able to describe types of correlation.

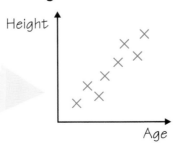

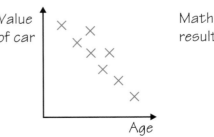

Positive correlation — this is when as one value increases so does the other.

Negative correlation — this is when as one value increases the other decreases.

Zero correlation — this is when there is no connection between the values.

Drawing scatter diagrams

- Work out the scales first before starting. Plot the points carefully, ticking off each point in the table as it is plotted.

Example

The data shows the age of several cars and how much they are now worth.

AGE (years)	1	8	4	7	6	3	5	7	3	5	2
PRICE (£)	5200	1200	3400	1800	2800	4000	1800	2400	4400	3000	5000

Plot the points carefully since it is easy to make mistakes.

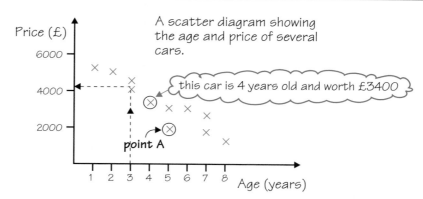

A scatter diagram showing the age and price of several cars.

this car is 4 years old and worth £3400

point A

- The scatter diagram shows that the older the cars become the less they are worth, i.e. there is a **negative correlation**.

- **Point A** shows a car which is 5 years old and worth £1800. This is slightly less than expected and may be due to rust or a dent, etc.

You need to be able to interpret the scatter diagram.

Misleading graphs

- Statistical graphs are sometimes misleading, they do not tell the true story.

Examples

In the exam make any criticisms clear.

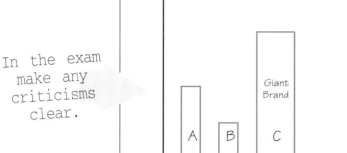

This graph is misleading because it has no scales and the bars are not the same width.

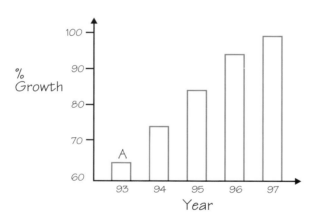

This graph is misleading because the scales do not start at zero, so the growth looks much bigger than it actually is.

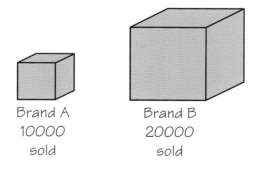

This pictogram is misleading because the pictures change size. Although Brand B has only sold twice the amount of Brand A it gives the impression of having sold much more.

Averages

There are three types of averages: **mean**, **median** and the **mode**.

Mean – sometimes known as the 'average'

$$\text{Mean} = \frac{\text{sum of a set of values}}{\text{the number of values used}}.$$

Median – the middle value when the numbers are put in order of size.

Mode – the one that occurs the most often.

Range – this tells us how much the information is spread.

Range = highest value – lowest value.

Example

A football team scored the following number of goals in their first ten matches:

2, 4, 0, 1, 2, 2, 3, 6, 2, 4.

Find the mean, median, mode and range of the number of goals scored.

$$\text{Mean} = \frac{2 + 4 + 0 + 1 + 2 + 2 + 3 + 6 + 2 + 4}{10} = \frac{26}{10} = 2.6 \text{ goals.}$$

Do not round off.

Median = 0, 1, 2, 2, 2, 2, 3, 4, 4, 6   Put in order of size first.

0̸ 1̸ 2̸ 2̸ ⟨2 2⟩ 3̸ 4̸ 4̸ 6̸   Cross off from the ends to find the middle.

$$\frac{2 + 2}{2} = 2 \text{ goals.}$$

If there are two numbers in the middle the median is halfway between them.

Mode = 2 goals, because it occurs 4 times.

Range = 6 – 0 = 6.

Remember to subtract the two values in order to obtain the range.

Finding averages from a frequency table

- A frequency table tells us **how many** are in a group.

Example

Charlotte made this frequency table for the number of minutes late students were to registration:

Number of minutes late (x)	0	1	2	3	4
Frequency (f)	10	4	6	3	2

This tells us that 4 students were 1 minute late for registration.

Two students were four minutes late.

Mean $= \dfrac{\text{Total of the results when multiplied}}{\text{Total of the frequency}}$

$= \dfrac{(10 \times 0) + (4 \times 1) + (6 \times 2) + (3 \times 3) + (2 \times 4)}{(10 + 4 + 6 + 3 + 2)}$

$= \dfrac{0 + 4 + 12 + 9 + 8}{25} = \dfrac{33}{25} = 1.32$ minutes late.

Remember to add up the total frequency.

Median

There are 25 students in the class, the middle person is the 13th.

From the frequency table:

Number of minutes late (x)	0	1	2	3	4
Frequency (f)	10	4	6	3	2

the first 10 students

the 13th student is in here.

Median number of minutes late is 1.

Mode

This is the one that has the highest frequency.

Mode = 0 minutes late because it had a frequency higher than any others.

Range $= 4 - 0 = 4$ minutes.

Remember to write down the answer zero, not the number 10 (this is the frequency).

Comparing sets of data

• The range and averages are used to compare sets of data.

Example

9A obtained a mean of 57% in a test.

9T obtained a mean of 84% in the same test.

From the averages we would say 9T is better than 9A. However if the range is looked at for each class:

9A = 100% − 21% = 79%.

9T = 94% − 76% = 18%.

Using the range it can be seen that not all of 9T are better than 9A, because some of 9A obtained higher marks than 9T. The average for 9A has been lowered because of the low marks obtained by some pupils.

Use the range when comparing data.

Processing and interpreting data

Questions

1 A chocolate firm asked 1440 students which type of chocolate they preferred. The pie chart shows the results. How many people preferred:

(a) White chocolate?

(b) Fruit and nut?

(c) Milk chocolate?

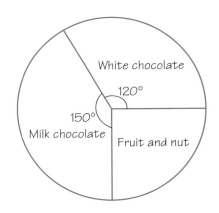

2 Look at the two graphs below.

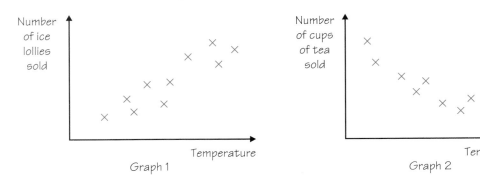

Graph 1

Graph 2

(a) What does graph 1 tell you about the relationship between the number of ice lollies sold and the temperature?

(b) What does graph 2 tell you about the relationship between the number of cups of tea sold and the temperature?

3 Using the histogram opposite, complete the frequency table below.

(a)

Thumb lengths (cm)	Frequency
$2 \leq L < 4$	
$4 \leq L < 6$	
$6 \leq L < 8$	7
$8 \leq L < 10$	
$10 \leq L < 12$	

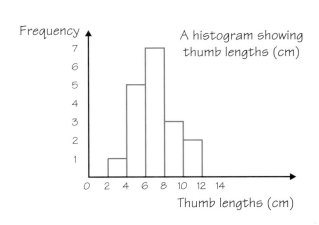

(b) How many people were in the survey?

(c) Draw a frequency polygon on the histogram.

4 Find the mean, median, mode and range of this data:

2, 4, 1, 1, 2, 3, 7, 5, 5, 5, 2, 5, 6.

5 The number of sisters that each student in class 9M has are recorded in the table below:

Number of sisters (x)	0	1	2	3	4	5	6
Frequency (f)	7	9	4	4	2	2	1

(a) Calculate the mean number of sisters that the students have.

(b) What is the modal number of sisters?

6 This question was included in a survey. 'Do you agree that swimming lessons should only take place on a Saturday morning?' What is wrong with the question?

Estimating and calculating the probabilities of events

Probability

- This is the chance that something will happen.

- Probabilities must be written as either a **fraction**, **decimal** or **percentage**. **Never** write the words 'Out of'.

- Probabilities can be shown on a probability scale. All probabilities lie between 0 and 1. No event has a probability greater than 1.

Unlikely to happen   Very likely to happen

```
    |--------|--------|--------|
    0       0.5       1
```

definitely will not happen, i.e. I have 5 heads.

evens chance, i.e. obtaining a head on a fair coin.

definitely will happen, i.e. the sun will set today.

Example

A bag contains 3 red, 1 blue and 4 yellow beads. If a bead is chosen at random:

(a) Mark with an X the probability of choosing a green bead.
(b) Mark with a Y the probability of choosing a yellow bead.

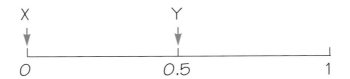

X is at 0 since there are no green beads, i.e. a green will definitely not be chosen.

A yellow bead has an evens chance of being chosen, since half of the beads are yellow.

Exhaustive events account for all possible outcomes, i.e. the list 1, 2, 3, 4, 5, 6 gives all possible outcomes when a fair die is thrown.

Probability in practice

- Estimates of probability can be carried out by experiment, surveys or symmetrical properties of the shape.

Example

It could be said that the next car to pass the school is blue only after a survey has been conducted.

Calculating probabilities

- Probabilities can be calculated using the fact that each outcome is equally likely.

Probability of an event = $\dfrac{\text{Number of ways an event can happen}}{\text{Total number of outcomes}}$

P (event) is the shortened way of writing the probability of an event.

Example

There are 12 socks in a drawer, 3 are red, 4 are blue and the rest are black. Nigel picks out a sock at random. What is the probability that the sock he has pulled out is:

(a) blue?   (b) red?   (c) black?   (d) blue, red or black?
(e) green?

Make sure that the number on the bottom is the total number of outcomes.

(a) $P(\text{blue}) = \frac{4}{12} = \frac{1}{3}$

(b) $P(\text{red}) = \frac{3}{12} = \frac{1}{4}$

(c) $P(\text{black}) = \frac{5}{12}$

(d) $P(\text{blue, red or black}) = \frac{12}{12} = 1$

(e) $P(\text{green}) = 0$

All probabilities add up to 1, i.e. choosing a blue, red or black sock will definitely happen.

There are no green socks in the drawer so the event will definitely not happen.

Probability of an event not happening

If two events cannot happen at the same time:

P(event will not happen) = 1 − P(event will happen)

To find the probability that an event will not happen:

- Find the probability the event will happen.
- Subtract it from 1.

Example

The probability that it rains today is $\frac{7}{11}$. What is the probability that it will not rain?

Use the fraction key on your calculator to help.

$P(\text{not rain}) = 1 − P(\text{will rain})$

$P(\text{not rain}) = 1 − \frac{7}{11} = \frac{4}{11}$.

Example

The probability that the torch works is 0.53. What is the probability that it does not work?

To quickly check add both numbers up and make sure you get 1.

$P(\text{does not work}) = 1 − P(\text{works})$

$P(\text{does not work}) = 1 − 0.53 = 0.47$.

Expected number

- Probability can be used to estimate the expected number of times an event is likely to occur.

Example

If a die is thrown 180 times, approximately how many two's am I likely to obtain?

Remember there are 6 outcomes on a die.

Since a 2 is expected $\frac{1}{6}$ of the time.

$P(2) = \frac{1}{6} \times 180 = 30$ two's.

Key in on the calculator: [1] [÷] [6] [×] [180] [=]

Example

The probability that Ellie obtains full marks on a spelling test is 0.4. If she takes 30 spelling tests in a year, in how many tests would you expect her to make no mistakes?

$0.4 \times 30 = 12$ tests.

Possible outcomes for two events

- Using lists, diagrams and tables are helpful when there are outcomes of two events.

- These tables are sometimes known as sample space diagrams.

Examples

For his lunch Matthew can choose a main course and a pudding.

List all the possible outcomes of his lunch.

Menu	
Main Courses	Puddings
Pizza	Apple pie
Chicken	Lemon tart
Salad	

Try and write out the outcomes in a well ordered way.

Pizza, Apple pie	Chicken, Apple pie	Salad, Apple pie
Pizza, Lemon tart	Chicken, Lemon tart	Salad, Lemon tart

There are 6 possible outcomes.

Example

The spinner and the die are thrown together, and their scores are added.

Represent the outcomes on a sample space diagram.

It may help to put a ring or square around the numbers you need.

- There are 18 outcomes.

  (a) The $P(\text{score of } 6) = \frac{3}{18} = \frac{1}{6}$.

  (b) The $P(\text{multiple of } 4) = \frac{5}{18}$.

Spinner

2	3	④	5	6	7	⑧
2	3	④	5	6	7	⑧
1	2	③	4	5	6	7

	1	2	3	4	5	6

Die

2 on the spinner, 6 on the die, 2 + 6 = 8

Estimating and calculating the probabilities of events

Questions

1 On the number line below place the arrows on the scale to show these probabilities:

(a) I will obtain a Head or Tail if I throw a fair coin.

(b) I will grow wings by 6 p.m. today.

(c) I will get an even number if I throw a fair die.

2 A bag has 3 red, 4 green and 10 yellow beads in it. If Reece takes out a bead at random, what is the probability that it is:

(a) a red bead   (b) a green bead   (c) a red or green bead   (d) a pink bead
(e) a red, green or yellow bead.

3 The probability that somebody leaves a message on an answering machine is 0.32. What is the probability that they do not leave a message?

4 The probability that Vali misses the bus is $\frac{7}{15}$. What is the probability that she does not miss the bus?

5 Kelly says that when she spins the spinner, the probability that she gets a 4 is 1/3. Why is she wrong?

6 The probability that you pass a driving test on the first attempt is 0.35. If 200 people are taking their driving test, how many would you expect to pass first time?

7 The diagram shows a two way table for pupils in a class, who are studying either Italian or Spanish.

	Male	Female	Total
Italian	5	10	15
Spanish	12	4	16
Total	17	14	31

(a) If a person is chosen at random, what is the probability that they do Spanish?

(b) If a girl is chosen at random, what is the probability that she does Italian?

8 A fair coin and a fair die are thrown together. Complete the sample space diagram below.

(a) What is the probability of getting a Head and a six?

(b) What is the probability of getting a Tail and an even number?

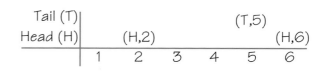

9 Two fair die are thrown together and their totals multiplied. Complete the sample space diagram.

(a) What is the probability of a total of 12?

(b) What is the probability that the total is a multiple of 4?

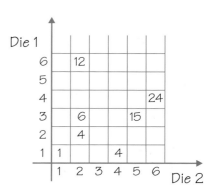

Answers

Place value and the number system

1 7 °C

2 A = 15   B = 4   C = −10   D = −20

3 (a) x = 24   (b) y = 25   (c) z = 152

4 19.4 kg, 19.04 kg, 6.302 kg, 6.032 kg, 2.74 kg, 2.7 kg

5 (a) 2 × 2 × 2 × 2 × 2   (b) 7 × 7 × 7   (c) 8 × 8 × 8 × 8

6 1.52×10^6

7 $\frac{6}{25}$

8 12%

9 (a) $0.\dot{7}$ 77.$\dot{7}$%   (b) $0.\dot{6}$ 66.$\dot{6}$%   (c) 0.6 60%   (d) 0.25 25%

10 6.49 (2 d.p.)

11 12.06 (2 d.p.)

12 9.5 (1 d.p.)

13 Three million, two hundred and forty eight thousand and twenty.

14 (a) 60   (b) 60   (c) 130

15 (a) 100   (b) 300   (c) 1400

16 (a) 7000   (b) 9000

Relationships between number and computation methods

1 (a) 20   (b) 26

2 (a) 6512   (b) 4181   (c) 22813   (d) 215

3 (a) 3, 6, 9, 12   (b) 2, 3, 5, 7, 11   (c) 1, 2, 4, 5, 10

4 (a) 8.8   (b) 21.54 (2 d.p.)

5 (a) 10   (b) 36   (c) 6   (d) 8

6 (a) 152   (b) 630   (c) 21000   (d) 0.252

7 £12.24

8 13

9 38.7% (1 d.p.)

10 £25.50

11 15

12 £200 Ahmed, £300 Fiona

Solving numerical problems

1 25.50

2 £10.83

3 2.8

4 The tin which costs 48p, is the better value.

5 2134

6 (a) 9 minutes   (b) 44 minutes

Functional relationships

1 (a) $n + 6$ (b) $p - 4$ (c) $3y + 6$ (d) $\frac{h}{7}$ (e) $\frac{n}{p} - 5$

2 (a) 13.2   (b) −26   (c) −25.2

3 $4n - 2$

4 $3n + 2$

5 A = (3, 2)   B = (1, 4)   C = (−2, 1)   D = (−5, 0)   E = (−3, −4)
   F = (2, −2)

6 (a), (b) See figure

    (c) y = 4x is steeper
       than y = 2x.
       They both pass
       through the origin.

    (d) See figure

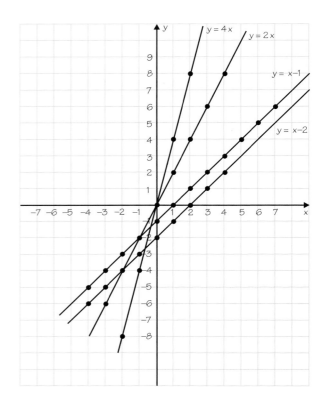

Equations and formulae

1 $S = 3P + 1$

2 (a) $10a$ (b) $6a + 3b$ (c) $5xy$ (d) $10ab$ (e) $12a^2$ (f) $6a + b$

3 $8a + 10b + 5$

4 Card C

5 (a) $a = 1$ (b) $n = 35$ (c) $n = 2$ (d) $n = 3$ (e) $n = -5$ (f) $n = -14$

6 9

7 105

Shape, space and measure

Properties of shapes

1

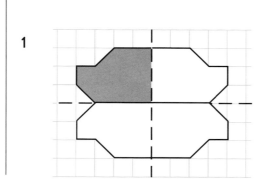

2 Hexagon

3

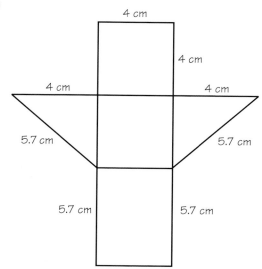

4 (a) a = 140°   (b) a = 100°, b = 80°, c = 80°   (c) x = 40°, y = 90°

(d) a = 50°, b = 130°, c = 50°, d = 50°

5 (a) Exterior = 60°   (b) Interior = 120°

Properties of position, movement and transformation

1 (a) 110°   (b) 240°   (c) 140°

2

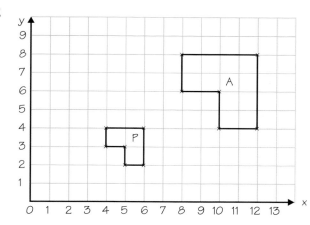

3 Forward 2. Turn right 90°. Forward 5. Turn right 90°. Forward 2. Turn right 90°. Forward 5

4

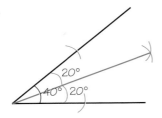

Measures

1 6.2 kg

2 42 mm

3 10.5 pints (approximately)

4 A = 9.2   B = 9.5   C = 2.42   D = 2.46   E = 2.48   F = 6.25

   G = 6.75

5 (a) 27 cm²   (b) 36 cm²   (c) 44 cm²   (d) 78.5 cm²

6 (a) 573.7 cm³   (b) 96.6 cm³

7 30.8 cm (1 d.p.)

Handling data

Processing and interpreting data

1 (a) 480   (b) 360   (c) 600

2 (a) As the temperature increases more ice lollies are sold (positive correlation)

   (b) As the temperature increases fewer cups of tea are sold (negative correlation)

3 (a)

Thumb length (cm)	Frequency
2 ≤ L < 4	1
4 ≤ L < 6	5
6 ≤ L < 8	7
8 ≤ L < 10	3
10 ≤ L < 12	2

(b) 18   (c)

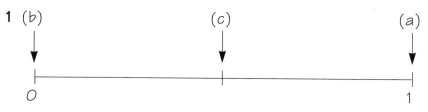

A histogram showing thumb lengths (cm)

4 Mean = 3.7 (1 d.p.), Median = 4, Mode = 5, Range = 6

5 (a) 1.83 sisters (2 d.p.)   (b) 1 sister

6 Your opinion that you want swimming lessons on a Saturday morning is evident

Estimating and calculating the probabilities of events

1

(b)   (c)   (a)

↓   ↓   ↓

├─────────────────────────────────┼─────────────────────────────────┤

0   1

2 (a) $\frac{3}{17}$ (b) $\frac{4}{17}$ (c) $\frac{7}{17}$ (d) 0   (e) $\frac{17}{17} = 1$

3 0.68

4 $\frac{8}{15}$

5 The outcomes are not equally likely, $P(4) = \frac{1}{2}$, as half of the spinner is a 4

6 70

7 (a) $\frac{16}{31}$ (b) $\frac{10}{14} = \frac{5}{7}$

8

Tail (T)	(T,1)	(T,2)	(T,3)	(T,4)	(T,5)	(T,6)
Head (H)	(H,1)	(H,2)	(H,3)	(H,4)	(H,4)	(H,6)
	1	2	3	4	5	6

(a) $\frac{1}{12}$ (b) $\frac{3}{12} = \frac{1}{4}$

9

Die 1

	1	2	3	4	5	6
6	6	12	18	24	30	36
5	5	10	15	20	25	30
4	4	8	12	16	20	24
3	3	6	9	12	15	18
2	2	4	6	8	10	12
1	1	2	3	4	5	6

Die 2

(a) $\frac{4}{36} = \frac{1}{9}$ (b) $\frac{15}{36} = \frac{5}{12}$

Index

This page can be used for your own notes